The Peace Angel

Nola tells the story of her extraordinary life with straight-on honesty. You see a frontier spirit coming out from the pages of her writing. What she says is startling: going to Heaven and speaking to God, multiple reincarnations, meeting souls she had known in previous centuries, becoming an angel here on earth. It has a fast-moving pace that still reads like a prayer.

—Thom Vines
Author of the award-winning *Tragedy and Trust* and *Hope's Ante*

The Peace Angel is one of those books that comes along occasionally and lands in your lap like a gift. A few pages in, you get that "buckle-up" feeling, and the book does not disappoint. This book makes you laugh, cry, and question the way you approach your own life. Empowering and thought-provoking.

—Lisa Doble
Senior Consultant in Counter-Terrorism, Security, and Resilience

Nola is a remarkable person and the honesty of her entire autobiography and beliefs shines through. I am totally impressed with her ability to overcome adversity and consistently and skillfully produce outstanding results. There are a number of powerful and positive messages in this book that many people would do well to take on board.

—Kelvin Glare, AO APM OStJ
Chief Commissioner, Victoria Police 1987–92

Your honesty throughout the pages moved me in a way I can't describe. It was like a movie playing before my eyes, and I did not want to stop reading. I was captivated throughout.

—Kate Stoupas (nee Sampson)
Documentary Filmmaker and Photographer

The Peace Angel

Taking Her Tears and Hanging Them Out To Dry

Nola Anne Hennessy

© 2014 Nola Anne Hennessy

All rights reserved. No part of this book may be used or reproduced by any means graphic, electronic or mechanical , including photocopying, recording, taping, or by any information storage retrieval system without the written permission of the publisher and author, except in the case of brief quotations which may be embodied in critical articles or reviews, with due reference to the source.

The Peace Angel

May be ordered through booksellers or direct from the publisher:

Serenidad Consulting Pty Ltd
PO Box 881
Sanctuary Cove QLD 4212
Australia

Ph: +61 7 55148077
Fax: +61 7 55148088
Email: enquiry@serenidadconsulting.com
www.serenidadconsulting.com/buy-our-books

ISBN 978-0-9874599-6-1 (sc)
ISBN 978-0-9874599-7-8 (hc)
ISBN 978-0-9874599-8-5 (e)

US Library of Congress Control Number: 2014939275

National Library of Australia CIP

Cover photography by Kate Stoupas (nee Sampson)
Cover design by Omar Mediano

Dedication

I dedicate my autobiography to:

God, for personally coming to me at just the right time.

Cousin Michelle, whose selfless acts continually help others.

My close and special Texas friends who have remained loyal and loving, some over many decades.

Dear friend Katie, with whom I still have a very special bond, now in its fifth decade.

My lovely, caring, and compassionate friends in the literary, sporting, and entertainment worlds.

Precious Nick, my courageous son.

And most notably, Jesse, the only man for whom I learned to feel true and forever love.

Yours truly and with love,

Ada

Preface

When I think about my life in total, a few simple yet powerful words come to mind: *amazing, creative, fabulous, great, moving,* and *motivating*. If I had not lived, I would certainly have been spared some immensely painful and soul-destroying experiences, yet I would not have come to know the joy of loving others unconditionally and the soul-nurturing power of total forgiveness; about working hard for what I want and need and seeing rewards for my efforts many times over; the pleasure of gaining unexpected public recognition for the philanthropic work I did quietly and without fanfare since age ten; that God does exist, that things happen in the right sequence, and for a reason; and that I am just one person in the bigger picture of humanity's journey.

My mother's death in February 2013 made me recognize in what seemed like a nanosecond that this autobiography had to be written now. To me, it was almost like my mother's living presence was preventing me from emptying myself of the residual memories and pain I had held onto at the deepest of soul levels despite all my past healing and the positive changes I had made in my life. I also felt her death signaled a new and open beginning where I could truly be free to be me.

The writing of this autobiography began as something I was doing for myself to gain full closure on my past—written for me, rather than for others. Before I started it and even half way through, I never thought that others would want or need to read it, or that it would ever see the light of day while I was alive. But something happened in the latter stages. The more I wrote in detail about what I'd learned and lived through, the more I began to think how maybe, just maybe, my life story might help someone else. It might even save someone's life or heal, inspire, or motivate someone. I felt something really good might come from its publication.

In the back of my mind had been the words my son Nick had said to me at the beginning of 2012, just before I sold my small ten-acre ranch and moved to the east coast of Australia to live by the sea. I sat with him at his apartment home in Canberra, on the couch, and shared my soul journey post-2002—explaining to him the key things I felt he needed to know to fully understand his mother's changes, and also that I really hadn't gone, rather that I'd been reborn. When I'd told him of my soul journey, going to Heaven, what I'd experienced, and that I wanted to write about it one day, he pondered all that for a while. He said he knew there would probably be people who won't be able to cope with it or even believe it, but there'll be a whole lot of people who'll want to hear my story, and it'll be really helpful for them.

I've come to realize there are probably as many different motivations as there are people who write, especially those who write nonfiction work that invokes strong emotion or tells a powerful story. I remember one day in late April 2013 I was sitting in the sun down at the foreshore park of the lovely beach close to my current home in Australia. I wanted somewhere away from home to write this—somewhere I could look up from time to time and see far into the distance. I was typing away on my laptop, totally absorbed in emptying my life into something that resembled a story, and up walked a woman wanting to have a chat.

I was gracious, of course, but I couldn't help thinking, *Can't you see I'm busy doing something on my computer? Why are you asking me if I'm working on something?* For the next twenty minutes after my thought flow had stopped and I'd ceased typing, and completely lost the brain-emptying mode I was in, all she could do was talk about how she would love to be able to sit by the beach and write her book.

What I received, without asking for it or even encouraging her, was an explosion of thoughts about how important her book was going to be, how she'd gathered all these facts and was going to expose people and how they'd live to regret it, how she'd be sure to get a movie deal, how people just had to know the real story, and how she was the only one to tell it. When she had finished talking about how her writing was so important, she turned to me and said, "What are you writing?"

"My autobiography actually."

She responded with a somewhat surprised tone, "What's so special about your life that you need to write about it?"

Shocked and a little annoyed, I replied, "Gosh, it's getting a bit chilly now. I think I'll head home. Good luck with your book."

I packed up my laptop, and as she started to move away, she turned back to me as she walked toward the beach surf life-saving clubhouse and yelled, "Sorry, I shouldn't have interrupted you!"

Well, that was an understatement, but what really struck me most about that time with her was her seeming disassociation that anyone else's life or story could be as important as hers.

That aspect of human nature, the selfishness and aloof egos of many people, disappoints me the most about humanity. I no longer have need of an ego. Ego is the one word to me that describes humanity's greatest barrier to a peaceful existence and total harmony for while people look first to fill their own ego cup, there is no room for giving to others.

I hope, as you read this story of my life thus far, in fact two spiritual lives in the one physical lifetime, that you can read between the lines and gain your own wisdom from my experiences. My story is just that—my story. Everyone on this earth has a story, some more painful and grotesque than mine, some far more illustrious and famous. Should you choose to tell your story one day, I salute you, for I know how tempting it can be to keep things to yourself or not value what you have or know or even who you are.

This writing experience has been the most courageous and hardest thing I've ever done in my life. It took me a full two weeks from late February 2013 to grow the inner strength needed to start penning it and to overcome my mother's programming that I should, no matter what, do as I'm told, even when doing as I was told meant living a lie, not advocating for change, or sticking up for myself enough.

I knew too, despite all the wisdom I'd gained throughout my life and being known as the consummate diplomat under immense pressure, that there were many people silently praying and hoping that my past would never be revealed. Some of these people will likely be shocked that they rated not a mention, others that they received only a cursory view. But after all, this is the story of my life as I have chosen for it to be written, in my own words. This final version is as true to me as the sun that rises every day, and I have shared only what I needed to share. The absence or inclusion of people in these pages, names changed where necessary, does not signal one way or the other their importance or lack of in my life. I have simply referred to and about those people in a manner that befits my relationship with them in my own words.

My first two books, *No Boxing Allowed* and *From Pre-Menstrual Syndrome to Positive Mental Attitude,* were specifically written to help others. This one was started for me. It was something I had longed to do for my soul's benefit since 2002, but the timing wasn't right. This time, almost like the final unwrapping of a dusty, weathered gift left wrapped and exposed to the elements for millennia, I am a soul poised ready to be completely exposed. Exposed and free, well and truly.

I hope you enjoy my story, and thank you, in advance, for having enough interest to do so. May your life be filled with priceless gifts, happy times, and soul-nurturing memories.

           Your friend in peace,
           Nola

Acknowledgments

For most authors, writing a book requires a degree of isolation, contemplation, reflection, and compromise. We sacrifice many things to bring a book to fruition as the primary creator of the work, but both behind the scenes and in direct support of our efforts, there are usually others who are essential to the process.

For me, writing this autobiography required me to be absent from my son Nick for lengthy periods, at a time when he and I were undergoing significant emotional transition. Words cannot really express how grateful I am that he understood my need for distancing myself from everyone in order to accomplish what I did. Second, Cynthia Brian, thank you for encouraging me to share my story with a wider audience; your compassionate review of an early manuscript version; your compassion and understanding during our many interviews, especially the March 2013 one which was taped at exactly the same time as my mother's funeral; and your friendship. Thank you also to Heather and Peter Turner for giving me time out from writing, by inviting me to stay overnight at their gorgeous Queensland retreat and taking me far into the Gold Coast Hinterland, one of the earth's best-kept natural resources.

To the small group of friends and colleagues I approached to read this and provide comments of endorsement, thank you all for your candor, patience, and responsiveness. And last but by no means least, a big thank you to Omar Mediano for the time taken to understand my sentiments about how my autobiography could be presented and devising such a thoughtful cover design.

Chapter 1

My birth early in the morning of June 17, 1957, was relatively uneventful for me on a physical level, yet I later came to remember the disengaging and hurtful words my mother spoke during that process and the passage of intense darkness that led to life outside the womb and being well and truly "in the light."

My childhood years, including infancy and toddlerhood, were a mixture of nurturing love, fun, and laughter; strong and emotional detachment; painful absence; cruelty; physical and emotional abuse; and sacrifice/denial and supreme levels of control. Those seem like a lot of conflicts for a youngster and especially for an infant/toddler to experience. They were.

For all of my life, my mother spoke ill of my father, even after he died in 1991. I always knew she had some unresolved feelings, had always kept her wedding ring, and cried that day I told her of his death. I always took my mother's side though—always figured what she told me was the truth. When you idolize your mother and keep forgiving the indelicate and harsh ways she handles you in life, it is hard to see that she could do any wrong. I could see my mother was always working; I couldn't understand why she didn't spend much, if any, social time with me when she was off work, but I accepted this as my life and just kept on looking for and finding the joyful aspects day by day, week by week.

From what I was told and understand, my mother and father married when she was twenty-one and he thirty-eight. This was his second marriage, and they had diametrically opposed political views—she, a left wing bordering on being a Communist and very rigid in her thinking and aggressive in her vocalizing and he, a right-wing capitalist focused on wealth creation.

Dad was a master painter and decorator—very particular about everything, good at what he did, and a heavy smoker of unfiltered cigarettes. They married around late 1951 to early 1952, and I was born in June 1957. What happened between them until I was born, I don't know much about, but I was told by a few relatives that there was trouble and a lot of arguments. My mother claimed to me that she had a kettle full of boiling water thrown over her by my father when she was pregnant with me, and while she was pregnant with me, they separated. When my father died, his death certificate stated he died "married." To me, that meant that he must have still been married to my mother, as I distinctly remember when he and I reunited in 1976 that he told me he had never married again after being married to my mother.

In early March 2013, my eldest uncle told me a story from the day their divorce hearing was held. The story now raises a question in my mind about whether Dad ever remarried or, if not, did he even know he was divorced? He wasn't present at the divorce hearing, so did he know the outcome or simply lose all recollection of the day? Surely his family with him in later years would have known? From all accounts, their marriage was doomed before it even got started—big age difference, opposite political views, and controlling, strong-willed, and temper-driven individuals. It was a short-lived marriage or coresidency, six to seven years, if that.

One heart-warming aspect of my childhood was the fairly frequent visits to see my grandparents at Sussex Inlet. That was my ultimate peace haven for the first twenty-one years of my life—on the water, quiet, relaxing, clean, welcoming, with loads of fishing and swimming. I would visit my grandparents during my annual school breaks and even as a young adult I drove to see them to be around them, feel their love, and experience the tranquility of their environment.

My grandparents taught me the value of giving to communities as a volunteer. From age ten, I was actively involved during every school holiday: helping Pa with his responsibilities as the president of the local Progress Association, selling tickets for "housie," making cakes and candies for fund-raising, helping Grandma set up stalls at markets, and decorating floats for processions. The activities seemed endless and were so much fun. It felt right and normal to volunteer to help others.

Whenever my mother had to come with us on holiday in Sussex Inlet, my duty was to share sleeping arrangements with her. Others had their own beds, but there I was stuck with a woman who snored, smelt really bad, always sweated, was significantly overweight, and generally was distasteful to be around, especially in the middle of the night when rest is so important. There was no privacy at all from her.

To some extent, I think my mother was jealous of me; even when I was a child, she was always looking at me in a way that was more like looking through me. She always intruded on my personal space. Whether it was to come in when I was dressing and then stand looking at me or regularly coming into my then master bedroom when I was married, she would sit down on the end of the bed and talk nonstop or simply stand and watch what was going on. She would also walk into my son's bedroom unannounced, and then take over or intrude on whatever was going on at the time—dressing him for bed, doing homework, or making the bed. She was present in such a way that it interrupted. She pushed her presence on people. She was a selfish woman in many respects, but that behavior in which she interrupted others' privacy was particularly strange. She was almost infantile in her manner, and unashamedly presumptuous about how welcome she was in someone else's personal space.

Whenever I visited Grandma and Pa on my own, it was the best time of all. I felt totally safe and not as controlled. Grandma never made me bathe with anyone else. Even with scarce quantities of rainwater collected in a tank outside, she always managed to have enough water for private baths. My grandparents had had one daughter and three sons, and I know for a fact that Grandma kept their activities and tasks pretty separate as they were being raised. It wasn't so much sexist segregation—it was more about the era when kids were raised and treated according to their gender. My mother often told me during her life that her childhood had been "just awful"—never being allowed to play outside with the brothers and always having to cook and clean while they were having fun. Even when my Grandma was gravely ill, the only thing my mother kept saying was how much she thought Grandma had been a bitch to her. How come I never saw that side of my Grandma? One person, viewed so differently by two people so close, could not have been such a Doctor Jekyll and Mister Hyde!

I saw my Grandma and the loving way she would caress Pa. I felt her loving touch, tasted the love in her food, and smelled the love and care in her hugs and clean home. That kind of good karma never comes from a "bitch." What my mother didn't realize was that she did to me tenfold or more in a worse way what her own mother supposedly did to her. If what my mother said is in any way true of her life as a child, then she repeated the mistakes and exacerbated their impact instead of breaking the familial pattern.

My maternal grandfather, Pa, was so left-wing he was nearly jailed for his political efforts. He was born in 1909, and Grandma was born in 1907. Pa was only a few years older than my dad, and their similar ages created some tension—especially knowing my grandfather as I did and how paternal he was about his family and others he cared about. Grandma never really said much about Dad that I can recall. She was always what I remember in my childhood days as being loving, cuddly, gentle, soft, and smelling like lily-of-the-valley flowers. I felt I could rely on her no matter what. She always seemed to be in the right place at the right time through my early and later years, and there are many pictures of me at their Sydney home riding tricycles or sitting in a pram. My heart is warm when I remember their homes and how Grandma and Pa were with me.

In those early days with them, my personality really started to come out. I was strong-willed, yet I recall feeling playful and free-spirited pretty much all the time around them. I know I used to giggle and laugh a lot, and I remember Grandma saying, "You're an angel when you're asleep." I was never malicious or negatively premeditated in anything I ever did that seemed fun, but I guess having fun was far more important to me than being a sit-around frump. Grandma always watched over what I was doing; Pa was the never-to-be-questioned wise one. I remember wanting to explore everything and everywhere. I still have that yearning in me at fifty-six and will probably never stop searching for and exploring new things and places to feed my brain and give me new experiences to learn and grow from.

All in all, I think I was probably a fair handful for Grandma. I remember always wanting to be in her good books, and I never deliberately put a foot wrong or got up to mischief. I know I probably did, in their eyes, get up to mischief—exploring and questioning a lot of the time, and sometimes coming back to their house after curfew had passed. There was always so much to explore where they lived at the coast. When I did get into trouble, I'd respond with a look that she described as the "bulldozer lip." Grandma would tell me, "Don't look like that—a cold wind might come along and freeze your face that way!"

I remember as a toddler being told one day by my grandfather, "Don't come down the back." I just knew he was going to get a "chook" for dinner—he used to have a henhouse around the back of his big shed at the back of the property, and miraculously these freshly caught hens would get converted into roast chicken for dinner that Sunday night. I'm not sure whether he plucked the feathers or Grandma did it, but there were always fresh eggs and roast chickens for us to enjoy. The day Pa told me not to follow, I was just too inquisitive not to. I followed at a distance, and I crept quietly down to the back corner of the shed to peer around and have a look at what my Pa was doing. There I saw it—axe in one hand, chook in the other hand. I was fascinated, especially because Pa only had one thumb; it must have been awkward for him to hold things. The poor chook didn't stand a chance. I can remember the bright red and shiny blood shooting out of what would have been the middle of its neck. The head was on the ground, motionless, yet the chook's body was still stumbling around like it still had a head. I remember thinking, How could that be? How can it walk around when its brain and head are gone? A bit like Professor Julius Sumner Miller on morning television in the 1960s saying, "Why is it so?"

Pa was annoyed with me for following him to the henhouse, but he was more concerned about the impact on me seeing an animal being decapitated. I don't recall receiving a smack, but I do remember his stern voice telling me I should do as I am told next time. Seeing the hen killed didn't do any harm to me at a psychological level. I never got nightmares. What it did do, though, was stir a feeling of wanting to understand anatomy and physiology, feelings that would resurface and be fulfilled many years later.

Pa and Grandma's houses always smelled what I call "right"—homely, comforting, and clean and fresh like timber; furniture polish; crisp, ironed linen; fresh-baked goodies; and a faint scent of fresh flowers. Grandma was the greatest and most loving cook. She always had cakes, special biscuits with icing, and everything freshly cooked from their abundant vegetable garden and eggs from the henhouse. Pa had been a greengrocer of sorts and had a selling stall at the Sydney produce markets for a while.

My infancy with them in Sydney was when I began my lifelong love of gardens filled with flowers and fresh vegetables, fruit, a clean home, and careful and love-filled cooking for the family and close friends. Pa once taught me how to pack fresh tomatoes into brown paper bags. When the bag was full, he taught me to gently but firmly hold the top corners while I threw the bag under and forwards to seal off the corners with a twist, and then close the top of the bag over the contents. I still do that to this day when I fill a paper bag. Their Sussex home would later become the next nurturing ground for my lessons in love, family, care, creativity, compassion, fishing, boating, prawning, and volunteer work for the community.

Chapter 2

When I was a toddler, and even later when I was in grade school, my mother used to take me into the central business district of Sydney. I was always fascinated by the hustle and bustle and loads to see and do. We used to go to David Jones's cafeteria, a store equivalent to Saks Fifth Avenue in terms of merchandise quality and style. I remember having one of two lunches—either smoked cod kedgeree, my favorite, or fried lamb's liver with grilled bacon in gravy. We also went to a cute soda/milkshake bar, and I always loved those city trips for the variety and outings they provided.

In every dress shop, I would climb onto the castor feet underneath the round dress racks and spin around the store. I guess I must have been bored or just looking for some fun. Mother always had me roped in leather reins whenever we went outside—literal reins, the kind that crisscrossed all over the body and had big silver buckles to strap me in. The reins had a long lead that she always held onto with a grip that was as hard as her smacks and looks of anger and contempt when I did something that displeased her.

When I think about how I felt at that time, I know I was working hard to have fun but at the same time to get away from her. In later years as an adult with my own toddler to care for, I could never imagine holding him back and restricting his freedom. Reins are cruel, and they certainly can have a negative impact on a child. The impact is exacerbated by a parent who is obviously more into being in control than being a loving mother and teaching in a gentler way. A child can be safe and close without having to be in bondage.

When I was around four, my mother took the family to live in Casino in northern, rural New South Wales (NSW). I don't have any substantial memories of the town other than a vague memory of the driveway of the house we lived in and the sparseness of the place—a bit of a dustbowl far away from civilization. The location was my first memory of deliberate physical cruelty being directed toward me by a member of my family. It was done via a tricycle or something similar. One or both of the tricycle's hard, rubber tires had come off the metal rims and was exposed and relatively sharp, able to cut or bruise anything in its path. My foot got in the road of one of the bare wheels and was badly damaged. However, it was the look in the person's eyes that shocked me the most—a cold, callous look like I could never imagine even on the worst monster's face.

Being so far away from Grandma and Pa during that period of time was just awful. I did not feel safe. I did not feel protected, loved, or nurtured. I didn't go to grade school, as I wasn't old enough. I do remember my mother was away for long periods during the day, and there always seemed to be babysitters and strangers around. I was always kept close-by and controlled.

Even after we returned to Sydney a few years later, and we began to live in Young Street Concord on what was then a very quiet street just up from Homebush railway station and bridge, there were still loads of minders, periods of her absence, and definite signs of the dysfunctional nature of my mother's lack of connection with me. I could not rationalize her behavior and attitude toward me then. I was still too young to fully realize and had this feeling of unconditional love that seemed to fix every bad memory in my head.

At the family home in Concord, I mostly played on my own. Most weekends, I would re-enact the hit TV show "Lost in Space" by pretending to play Mrs. Robinson of the Robinson family. I'd put thumbtacks in the back veranda posts and paint them red, yellow, and green to make spaceship control switches for the journey. I'd make mud pies, and I would serve them on the little plastic plates I had in my miniature tea set. I'd pick green leaves off the backyard trees—the fine leaves with tiny, petal-like fronds. I would wet them down to make "green veges" to have with the pies. I'd even paint rocks to look like potatoes and carrots, and many times played out the whole dining scene by eating the mud pie. That was a fun time, and even playing on my own I'd talk to the other members of my space family as we went on our adventures in outer space.

One of my aunts who married into the family always gave me books to read. Reading is a pastime I engaged in solidly for the first twenty-one years of my life and then later in my thirties and forties. My collection of books is now pure treasure, and all of those books I was given, with messages written inside, I still have to this day—Hans Christian Andersen, Robert Louis Stevenson, Shakespeare, and Sidney Dolten. One day, I plan to have them pass to my son and his children. They are real treasures that hopefully will be valued for many decades to come. Many wonderful and fancy, fun-filled stories filled my life with laughter and happiness beyond most people's comprehension.

To satisfy the artistic side of me that emerged quite young, I used to create and write plays to be acted out by my local district friends. I'd gather them together to sell the idea, teach them the scripts I'd written, help them with costumes and character styles, and finally bring them all together into the tiny, stuffy veranda spaces around the house at Concord to act out the plays. The lines were always punctuated with loads of laughter. Having my friends around and acting gave me a feeling of pure joy. No wonder in my final high school year book the caption under my picture reads "The Entertainer."

I shared a bedroom at Young Street Concord—a big bedroom in my eyes. The bedroom had an open fireplace that was never used with windows and foldout doors that led to a lattice-covered veranda area. The bedroom was at the end of a long hall, and the door was the tallest door I can ever remember walking through. Sharing a bedroom with someone of the other gender at the age of seven or so would not be ideal, but I remember thinking that having to share was like a kind of punishment to me for just being alive.

One time I remember having an absolute gutful of name-calling directed at me, and I made a comment back about that member of my family not being wanted. The response I got was a mixture of things, including being punched hard in the middle of the back. My only way of coping with off-handed and rejection-style actions, comments, and obvious anger and resentment towards me was to be playful and joke around quite a lot. But by being playful to compensate for silent treatment, the reactions I got were more of hatred and rage. I felt then a real sense of being unwanted. No matter what I did or didn't do, I always made certain people angry and physically violent. And the coping mechanism of mine, to say, "You're not wanted," came back to me as a karmic lesson over forty years later.

Living at Young Street Concord certainly draws a strong mixture of some very happy memories and many sad ones too. My mother worked away from the house, a dual-occupancy place she had bought. She rented out the smaller half of the duplex house to an older woman. This woman became my babysitter in the afternoons, and I remember she would bathe and feed me when my mother wasn't home in the evenings. The backyard was filled with trees to climb, lots of grass, and loads of room to run around. I remember many fun times in that backyard with the Frangipani trees and have many photos to show that life was good in many ways. However, the paling fences were so tall it seemed like a fortress. I always felt as if I were locked up and unable to have a view of life outside.

The feeling of the Young Street home being a fortress was a reality I faced for several years. Many of those memories of that time I "forgot" under hypnosis, but over the years the childhood memories I've needed, for my survival, protection, or ongoing happiness have been restored to my consciousness. Having these memories now will ensure I do not repeat the errors others or I made and will keep me safe from possible future harm.

Life in a small single-parent family was challenging. My mother was a working mother and away most of the time. The woman next door was our minder and that meant being at her house and bathed in the same bath at the same time as another family member. It was humiliating, embarrassing, and disgusting.

Money was obviously tight and an issue, but being accused by my mother of stealing the milkman's money that was left out every night when I knew I hadn't and never would was very hard for me to cope with. First, milk was my favorite drink. Second, Grandma and Pa had always taught me that "What is not yours, you do not take." I lost my allowance for months as punishment for something I hadn't done. However, I never received an apology or recompense of the allowance from my mother when the real thief was identified and caught red-handed. That was the hardest to take. My mother seemed to be so distant from me, and even though the truth was staring her in the face, she wouldn't give in and apologize. She wouldn't make the wrong that she'd done right. She was such a stubborn, strict, and cold woman so much of the time. The chubby and pushy European girl from down the road who always had lots of new costume, junk jewelry to show off and wear to Sunday school was the real thief.

Life in the Young Street home also meant not really having a healthy or sufficient diet of food. I was hungry a lot of the time, and my mother's idea of good cooking was something out of a can or reconstituted dried products. I rarely recall having fruit or vegetables except with my grandparents, but I do recall "Deb" Instant mashed potatoes, canned Irish stew, canned spaghetti in tomato sauce, lamb's fry and bacon, and lamb's brains and tripe. They were revolting and I was forced to eat them.

A real strong disappointment for me was being left alone at home when I was too sick to go to school with very little to eat but sufficient to drink to keep me going until my mother got home at some stage those nights. One of those times I was home alone I watched a Shirley Temple movie in black and white on TV. I was only seven, but I connected with her character in the movie. It touched me so deeply that it pivoted me in the direction of wanting to make things better for people, teaching receptive people a better way with relationships, and writing. Even at that young age, I knew I could one day make a difference.

One Sunday morning, I remember kicking a football in the backyard and slipping on the wet grass, having my feet come out from underneath me, and falling directly down onto my coccyx. I lost my voice for hours. I was chastised for not being careful instead of being comforted. The lack of comforting from my mother, who was always too busy with something else, was a soul-destroying and non-nurturing period that exacerbated the fear I had of being physically and verbally attacked and abused by others. Not feeling I could reach out to her and achieve a sense of understanding for the fear I felt and subsequent pain I endured with every incident was very hard.

One of the most emotionally damaging events was being left in hospital after my appendectomy operation at the age of ten. I had a severe appendicitis attack a couple of times and was taken for medical attention, but I was always treated like a burden to my mother. The doctor who operated on me was, as I found out later in recovery time, a trainee. He left a scar so large on my abdomen I thought it would never shrink. My mother visited me only once that I can remember. She was impatient, and I remember feeling alone a lot of the time I was hospitalized. On the funny flip side, I was very tall for my age, and I remember my legs used to dangle over the end of the children's ward bed that I was put into first. It was very obvious that the children's ward was not the place for me. The nurses finally moved me to an adult ward. I had more room there, loads more company, and other women patients who would ask me how I felt and if I was OK. That was nice; they really cared.

Dressing in second-hand clothes, except for what Grandma and Pa and other relatives gave me, was the start of my dread of birthdays and Christmas around my mother. Knowing that

I, and my later family, would be given something from a yard sale or a discount store as presents was traumatic. Never feeling valued or worthy enough to be given something new by her was emotionally damaging and deeply upsetting.

The start of some real trauma in my life came with my mother choosing a boyfriend, a real slimeball from Greece. He always touched me on the leg and wanted to hug me tight every time he came over to the house. I attempted to run away from home around that time so that I didn't have to put up with anymore of that life, him, or my mother. I was approaching adolescence, and I told my mother quite clearly, "If you marry him, I'll run away for good." I had told her about how he made me feel when he did his touching and hugging, but she had done nothing to protect me from his pedophilic ways. She must have thought I was lying—what a foolish woman!

One Saturday night, I remember my mother getting a phone call from him. She was all dressed up, and they were meant to go out somewhere. She hung up the phone and cried. This was the first time I'd ever seen my mother cry, and I was mad at him for causing that but relieved at the same time. I hoped and prayed he would never come back, and he didn't that I can recall. Years later, my mother disclosed to me that she found out he had gone back to Greece and "became a homosexual"—full-blown pedophile more like it.

Some people say that disappointments come from having expectations. I believe we have a right to feel disappointed any time we want to because it's a natural and normal reaction to a situation or event. The event or situation creates the pain response. Pain is not a result of expectations per se. Some of my pain came from never being allowed to receive or own a doll as a young girl. Barbie dolls were forbidden. My mother, a strong feminist and more man-like than most feminists, considered Barbie dolls sexist. What a joke! She certainly had male-female barriers and anti-male issues and had absolutely no idea how dolls can help a child in so many ways, so my only companion toy for much of my formative years was an eyeless, cork-stuffed, fluffy, full-sized bunny rabbit. Well, not so fluffy after I vomited on it one night in bed when I had food poisoning. The bunny ended up in the old washing machine tub being boiled to death to get rid of the smell.

Just before we left the Concord home and after pleading for what must have been years, I was finally given a doll that had a hole in its mouth and a hole in between its legs. The doll came with a bottle that could be filled with water and a pretend diaper for catching the water. I was in my element when I finally had a doll to hold, feed, and nurse—but only when mother would allow it. I was being rationed in my exposure to something that should be part of a child's normal development.

Worst of all, so many Christmas mornings I would wake up to find nothing under the tree, if there was a tree at all, or in a stocking. In the childhood years I believed in Santa Claus that day of the year was one I kept a light of hope for. Maybe Santa would reward me for being good. A Christmas stocking was a pillowcase wrapped over the back of a kitchen chair, and sometimes there was no pillowcase at all. My mother was always so tired and sleeping. We put reindeer and Santa food and drink out in the kitchen. One Christmas morning I remember waking my mother up gently and asking "Did Santa come? There aren't any pressies." She told me to go away and come back later. I thought for so long, *But I haven't been bad. Why am I being punished by Santa?* I came to realize fairly soon that mother was "Santa."

I compensated for that lack of childhood comfort toys by buying myself my own brand-new teddy bear in 2003. I still have that gorgeous little bear sitting on one of the guest beds at my current home. He was my gift to me to help complete the cycle of my former life, rounding off the aspects of my childhood that had not been fulfilled properly. He is something for me to treasure and share the fun of with loved ones and visitors.

Decades later, I came to realize and accept that despite all the lack of new gifts, nutritious food, warmth, and mother-comfort, there was always plenty of money for my mother's wardrobe of clothes and shoes, nightclub dance outings, and political party activities. The secondhand gifts; old clothes; feeling cold and hungry; not having enough money to go on most school excursions during the early years prior to when I started to earn my own income at age twelve; feeling deprived of validation as a human being worthy of love from its mother—all of these experiences created strong feelings of inequality in me from a very young age. I had to work hard all my working and personal life to achieve a sense of self-worth through relationships, my career climbs, and seemingly endless setbacks. Only in the last five years or so, with all that I have been through spiritually and emotionally, could I safely and confidently validate myself. I've learned to give love to myself where others withhold it, and I value myself for being a woman of goodness, real chastity, virtue, honesty, and unconditional love. I know myself to be a giving and compassionate woman of integrity and forgiveness.

I am a "happy little vegemite" by nature and owe it to the loving members of my family and friends to now share the upside to all of those negatives at Young Street Concord. There were a significant number of pluses, and I had fun and made many happy memories along the way.

Chapter 3

Religious education and activity was something many of my wider family partook of and yet, for my own immediate family unit, going to church or Sunday school was not the norm. Although I don't recall how it came to be, I had the chance several times during that time at Concord to go to Sunday school up the road a ways to make new friends and experience life outside the house. I felt welcomed and valued by the church, and, to this day, the times I go into a church for a wedding or funeral, I always feel completely at ease. For me, going to Sunday school as a child was more about connecting to a God I didn't really know for sure existed and also being open to receiving the messages of the particular church without prejudice in my heart. Being spiritual was something I knew about myself, but I didn't have a way of describing it, and I didn't really need to until much later in my life.

One really lovely event that occurred in my life around the time we moved back from Casino around 1963–64 was meeting Poncie Ponce, the American star of *Hawaiian Eye*. I remember it was hot and muggy, and we met at a ten-pin bowling alley on the Gold Coast in Queensland, a famous place for glitzy glamour and fun. I knew straightaway who he was, and Poncie was really nice to me. He was talkative and attentive and even showed me how to bowl a ball down the alley properly. Poncie was one of many stars I would come to meet in my lifetime and, like all the others, so pleasant and friendly when he could have so easily dismissed me, being such a big star at the time.

One of my favorite activities was putting pennies on the Homebush railway line down the end of the street. Although it was a highly dangerous activity, I wanted to see what a penny would look like after being flattened by a train wheel! That was, of course, before February 1966 when Australia converted from pounds, shillings, and pence to dollars and cents. Another favorite activity was traveling the long bus ride up a busy main road, Parramatta Road, to Haberfield Demonstration School in Sydney. I went to school there from grade two to halfway through grade six. We moved away from Sydney just before my eleventh birthday.

I was always a year younger than everyone else at school. Only my mother knows why she insisted I start school so young, and I knew that she pulled strings. The cut-off birthday for school entry at Haberfield was May at that time, so when kids would normally turn seven in the first year of grade school, I turned six. Being up to eighteen months younger than most kids in the same year at school was always a challenge and in later high school years very difficult for me to feel like part of the older group. I had to work hard to be accepted.

I loved spending my three pence of pocket money each week on a big bag of candy lollies from the milk bar. I'd get off the bus at the bottom of the hill from school, buy the candies, and then share them with all my friends at school throughout the day. But not everyone in my life had the same desire to give. I came to see how greed and lack of sharing can completely overwhelm some people in my family. I was giving for giving's sake, not to receive in return.

When the new-wave television came to Australia, it was quite a while before we had a set in our house. But when it came, I rejoiced—our own black-and-white TV to watch. I had waited so long. We always had a wireless radio and listening was good, but the moving pictures were everything and beyond to satisfy my imagination of worlds and people far away. I loved watching the original *Disneyland* on TV on a Sunday evening. Watching cartoons and shows like Abbott and Costello, though I never liked the hitting; the Flintstones; the Jetsons; the Dean Martin Show and his movies with Jerry Lewis; John Wayne movies; Fred Astaire and Ginger Rogers musicals; and old black-and-white romance movies. So much of Australian TV in the 60s was American. I just loved it.

Just before we moved to Canberra when I was ten, I was sent to Bateau Bay National Fitness Camp run by the NSW Department of Education in the summer holidays of year five of grade school. Getting away from home, sleeping out under the stars on bivouac, singing songs by the campfire, and learning survival skills in the wild helped me to cope with my life at home. Yet there were some yucky girls who were hellbent on making my life miserable. I made the most of the time away despite the negatives and lapped up the sense of freedom that being outdoors created.

Haberfield Demonstration School was the school that really molded the student of learning and self-motivation aspects of me. Haberfield was a teaching school, one that my mother identified as a school that could potentially provide the best level of public education for her children. It was exclusive in whom it took, co-educational yet segregated. Boys and girls were classed separately and were separated in the playground most of the time as well. Most of the photos I have of that time show all-girl classes, yet the year photos were co-ed.

I had one real friend, Louise Devine, and there was also one young girl that I always had trouble with. She would turn out to be quite a number later in life—very ego focused and in the media for one scandal after another. She was a real tomboy type, incredibly aggressive, from a very affluent family I understand, full of herself, and always pushing to be in the spotlight at school.

I was getting pretty sick of being pushed around by that stage. One day, when she did something really awful to me that was completely humiliating, I picked up her school bag, walked down to Parramatta Road, and placed it neatly in the center of the traffic flow. I returned to school and did not say a word. When her bag was discovered that afternoon ripped and squashed on the road, she went into a rage. Arms were flinging, legs were kicking, and she was so mad that spit was coming from her mouth. I faced her and told her that I had put her bag there because she was so mean to me. I got a fat lip in return.

When I think about that punch in the mouth, it is not so much the punch and the swollen lip that I remember but the complete lack of lady-like manner she had about managing her emotions. Maybe I shouldn't have put her bag in the middle of the road, but it sure felt as if I was getting my own back, in a little way, for her being nasty to me so many times. I came to learn at the ripe age of nine that even if someone does something mean repeatedly, sometimes you need to turn your back and walk away. Her life became one of notoriety of the kind no decent and moral woman would seek, whereas mine became one of respect, trust, professional achievement, and a great deal of personal satisfaction. It took me just a short time to realize that getting back at someone isn't worth it in the big scheme of things. A point of compromise can be reached, and revenge is never a good route to take.

Haberfield was by far the strictest school I ever attended. We wore box-pleat, heavy drill uniforms, berets, heavy black tights, polished shoes, actual men's ties, crisp white shirts, fine-spun gloves, and school insignia badges. It was a bit like a military school. We would march around the playground area in school class years, and then march in two lines up the stairs into the school building to class.

Around the classroom walls, there were always samples of student work. Student teachers lined the back and two sidewalls of the classrooms to watch, listen, and learn from both the experienced teacher out front and the students themselves. Classroom-style learning can be challenging enough, mixed or same gender, and adding the pressure of having wall-to-wall student teachers meant it sometimes became quite challenging. Everyone was on show, every day, all the time. If you set a foot wrong, it was detention for the girls and the cane for the boys. Class might as well have been boot camp for all I could see, but it did teach me pride in how I looked and in my school.

At morning recess, we drank our third pint of almost sour, warmed-in-the-sun milk. The cream had settled on the top and turned yellow by the time we came out for recess playtime. From that time on, regardless of whether milk came in glass bottles, cardboard UHT boxes, or plastic bottles, I've always shaken the container to mix the milk with the cream. I still do it to this very day but only with full-cream milk, which I rarely drink. Some old habits die hard.

One very good aspect of my life in Sydney was being able to travel into the heart of the city on a Saturday morning to play competition netball. Sometimes I remember not wanting to go, but I'm glad for the routine and healthy level of fitness it gave me. I'm not sure if my mother paid for that or made it happen or not, so I don't know whom to thank. It could have been my Dad's idea, not that it really matters now.

I also went to ballet and tap dancing classes for a couple of years and remember, with much enjoyment, dancing around in my tap shoes on the cement under the back veranda of the house on Young Street Concord. I became my own little Shirley

Temple and loved every minute of it. At some stage, I learned Scottish sword dancing and became quite good at that too. All of those lessons paid off when I was given an important part in a live production run at Sydney's Town Hall. I had the part of a young girl who had to dramatically run across the width of the stage. The role was intense, and I loved it. The role brought out the best in me until my later singing part in Gilbert and Sullivan's *Mikado*. I played Pitti-Sing and really nailed it.

I had the joy of taking in a sick dog once, much to my mother's resistance. I remember his lovely face, his lapping up my care and attention, and his gentle way with me.

The one and only time Louise was allowed by my mother to come and visit at my home was a real treat. We had a pajama party, and it was so much fun. We were only about seven, but I remember we had a bubble bath together in the tiny square bath beneath the shower in our one small family bathroom and laughed and splashed about like mermaids. Louise was my best friend, and we were more like sisters than friends. She was so pretty and feminine. We were so in tune and so sure that we would each marry a tall, dark-haired, and handsome man one day. We never saw each other again after I left Sydney in 1968, and I missed her friendship for a long time.

As well as bringing a few years of stability, Sydney life in the early 1960s brought a variety of events, including moving. It seemed to me like we were always moving from one house to another, and in fact, we were. On the upside, living opposite Bob and Dolly Dyer of BP Pick-a-Box fame was the most exciting.

During that time in Sydney we were always going to TV stations for one thing or another. I met many TV, music, and radio stars as a result of some TV game shows that my mother went on in the sixties—Lucky Star, Col Joy and the Joy Boys, Little Patty the singer, Jimmy Hannan, Ugly Dave Gray, Noelene Brown, Tommy Hanlon Jr., Graham Kennedy, Stuart Wagstaff, Bobby Limb, Dawn Lake, and Barry Crocker, just to name a few. I had a little autograph book, and by the end of those visits to the TV studios and other events, the book was full of autographs and my head full of memories. When I moved to the USA to live in 1981, the book stayed packed in a box at my mother's place. I never saw that autograph book again.

One of the TV stars we met became friends with my mother, so much so that we went to the beach for outings. Johnny took me on his surfboard out beyond the breakers and, for the first and only time in my life, I sat on his shoulders while he surfed. I didn't enjoy the experience as I couldn't swim well. I was terrified of being out of my depth having been deliberately pushed into a swimming pool when I was younger and nearly drowning. I'd also been on a sandbar at Coogee Beach when it unexpectedly collapsed and hundreds of people were suddenly in the deep water and screaming. Mostly I didn't like sharks, but it was cool to be surfing with a TV star.

My mother herself didn't provide a feeling of emotional or physical stability for me most of the time, and this rubbed off on me so much so that by the time I moved to Texas to start a new life in 1981, I was well and truly craving settling down somewhere I could call home.

Chapter 4

The family's move to Canberra in May 1968 was a huge turning point for me. Moving away from my friends and school and going from warm temperate Sydney to the cold, sometimes harsh and dry Canberra was a huge change. I think my mother moved for better work opportunities. The level of daughter-as-housekeeper duties was on the incline. I'd been made to clean from around ten years of age, and the older I got, the more I was told to do. In many respects, though, the move was the launch of new things for me. Over time, I would come to realize the changes that were occurring were signaling other changes and events that would occur later in my life. My spiritual receptivity has been pretty high all my life, and, even as an adolescent, I was honing that skill without even knowing it at the time.

The family initially moved to a bed and breakfast for a couple of weeks. We then moved to a place called Tall Trees Guest House in an inner suburb of the city. It was a guesthouse frequented largely by Australian National University students, and the rooms were pretty much like a motel with a common lounge at the front of the building. Here is where I observed the young men and their lady-friends-for-the-evening and thought, *If I'm to be taken seriously, I'll have to smoke cigarettes.*

I started to smoke. I was sneaking back into the common lounge after everyone had gone to bed, finding half-smoked cigarettes in ashtrays, finding matches, and lighting up. I was only ten. After about two weeks of coughing and spluttering, just around my eleventh birthday, my mother smelled cigarettes on my breath. The wooden coat hanger that was in her closet very quickly changed to being a whip for the back of my legs. I couldn't bend my legs for days after that without intense pain. The welts were enormous, and all the while I thought, *That won't make me stop. Hitting me won't change my behavior or choices. All you did was hurt me.*

After Tall Trees, we moved to so many residential locations I couldn't keep count. We lived in one apartment-style place the year I caught chicken pox, and I was also attacked by magpies while I crossed a park to get to the school bus. The birds took two big chunks out of my scalp which left me bleeding badly—what an unpleasant time that was. We lived in a cheap, dirty unit in Queanbeyan, a small satellite city of Canberra. Catching the public transport bus to school each day and back was horrific. I couldn't breathe for the bad body odor coming from some of the southern European and English people on the bus. The air was so thick with their breath and odor I would dry-retch most mornings on the way to school. Then we moved to a suburb called Hackett—very leafy and pleasant.

I had an hour bicycle ride to high school, but it was an OK location nonetheless. While living in Hackett, I began saving twenty cents a week to buy a pack of ten full-strength Marlboro Red cigarettes. My mother may have known I smoked, but she never beat me again after the Tall Trees incident. Maybe I said something or went silent with shock. Whatever the reason, I smoked, and it felt good and gave me a sense of owning my own destiny—being in control of my choices.

I loved the bike ride to school and being by myself and free to stop. I could listen to sounds and smell the roses. My home life at Hackett was not pleasant a lot of the time—a mixture of silent treatment, distancing, and other bullying. From those early teenage years, I never bothered challenging my mother because as far as I could see, I was being blamed, every time, regardless of any fact presented to her. I seemed to be the easy scapegoat for other people's inadequacies and biases.

From age ten, living in Sydney and also in each new residence in Canberra, the load of household chores fell to me. I felt like a slave. Effectively that is what I was—a free labor resource, captive in the home, for my mother to use at will. I really felt, and was, used.

For nearly ten years, from ten to nineteen until I could finally escape to another city, I did what my mother was too lazy or unwilling to do. Her choice not to clean her own home, bathe herself regularly, or wash her own dishes continued on after I married and had my own family responsibilities. When she lived on her own, her house was never clean and welcoming. For well over twenty years, she lived with removal boxes fully or partly packed in anticipation of moving. She stacked these boxes under beds, inside closets, in the kitchen, and in the living room. Everywhere boxes of stuff, filth, and dishes that had obviously been piled high for weeks attracted roaches and ants.

The contrast between my Grandma and my mother was so stark that the memory of those differences punctuated my life. It is only since my mother's death that I can say I am released from comparing the two and wondering why there were such huge differences. My grieving since her death has not been at all about missing her. I had no contact with her, by my actions and request for her to stay away from me, since December 2008. I had grieved her and come not to love her at all. My grieving was about what we'd never had, what we had missed out on.

By the time I turned twelve, I was legally able to get a job outside of school hours, pay income tax to the government, and be somewhat independent. My mother clearly welcomed my efforts at earning money for myself and encouraged it. I gathered that was because the more I earned, the less she felt she had to contribute to my upbringing. From age twelve, the new clothes I wore, the special food treats I bought, and the excursions I took were all funded by me. I continued to receive the secondhand clothes, be denied time with friends, and be prevented from visiting their homes on weekends. It was almost like she was forcing me to gain independence before I was ready, but then she kept me cooped up when it suited her interests. Her treatment made me grow up and get street-smart really fast. I was working long weekend and Friday-night hours in multiple jobs, getting migraines, and vomiting from all the pressure of school, work, and her expectations of me to do as well as others.

In the middle of my first year of high school, I was walking through a David Jones store after school and stopped at the record section. To my amazement and awe there was Bill Cosby flicking through LPs. I can still remember thinking *Oh, I wish I had my autograph book.* Instead I reached inside my school bag and pulled out one of my notebooks, moved toward him, and asked if I could have his autograph. Bill turned to me that day with the biggest smile on his face. He was such a tall and graceful-looking man with beautiful karma coming out of him. He was delighted to sign my notebook, and we engaged in conversation. He gave me my first real sense of being someone of priceless value.

Despite the negatives, I managed to achieve a whole bunch of things by the time I was in my early teens. I did well in many subjects at school. I made some nice friends, and did find a way to go to their homes after school some days when my mother was still at work. As I wrote in my first book, when the proverbial shit hits the fan, you usually pull yourself out of it better and stronger than before. High school was, by and large, a positive experience for me as a person, but it was coupled with intense feelings of inadequacy fostered by my mother's constant pressure.

With the first NASA walk on the moon by Neil Armstrong in 1969 came my first and only experience at "wagging," or skipping class. My best friend and I wagged high school for the afternoon to go to her house and watch the event on her TV. We watched that moon landing and walk together at her parents' home in Campbell, eating creamed corn on grilled cheese-on-toast, and drinking hot chocolate and milk. That was one of the best experiences of my life, that day sharing the monumental moon walk for humanity with her at her home. It was great knowing that I had witnessed a mark in history that would change humanity forever. She remained a friend for the next three years, but as I began to withdraw and feel incredibly insecure in myself and how well I was doing in life, I moved toward some other friends for the last couple of years in high school.

Many of the early years for me at high school were marked with boys keeping their distance and staring and, at times, a few being really horrible. After I turned thirteen and had been kissed for the first time at Sussex Inlet while on holidays at my grandparents' place, it was like they suddenly had license to be nasty. I couldn't work it out; every one of my girlfriends had boyfriends by fourteen, but none of the boys I was interested in, other than one from Sussex who wrote love letters to me for years and constantly sent me pictures of his life and Harley Davidson motorbikes, would give me the time of day except to wisecrack, make fun of me, or attempt to look up my dress as I traversed the stairs at school. At a thirty-year reunion in 2004, I confronted the men who as boys had been so nasty. I asked them why they had been real jerks, and unashamedly they admitted doing that because they liked me but were too afraid to step closer—pretty immature on their part.

During 1970 to 1972, I was in contact with the boy I met on holidays at Sussex. He was lovely and my first love interest. He sent me beautiful love letters that I kept for many years until I moved to Melbourne in 1978. We only ever kissed, hugged, held hands, wrote letters, and talked. That same year, I dated a very gifted swimmer in high school. He was my second official boyfriend. One night, with a full load of kids in his car, we headed off to a city motel to "muck around." I had no idea what was in store that night. Beneath the white sheets of the double bed in that motel room surrounded in the room by other boys and girls, I lost my virginity. Not an overly earth-breaking event for me but a key lesson—keep your sex activities private. I was mortified about having that happen in such a public setting.

By fifteen my mother had actually positioned me well for life ahead by insisting I attend a grooming and deportment course. I loved that course, and I remember walking with a book on my head so that I could learn to stand and walk straight with a degree of elegance. Always during my childhood, Mother was grabbing my shoulders from behind and reefing them back sharply. She would say, "Stand up straight, shoulders back." I guess she got sick of doing that, and she sent me to the class as a last, desperate attempt. What she didn't realize is that what I learned in that June Dally-Watkins class was the foundation for my later modeling and photographic work. I was grateful to her for that course, and when I think about it now, I wonder if that stooped-over look came from my mother's constant pushing of me and burdening me with too much too soon.

By fifteen, I had been working and earning a part-time income for three years. I had gone from being a sales assistant in various stores and cafes to being a supervisor of others, waitressing at weddings and other functions, and helping chefs prep for large functions. That was a fun part of my life—always getting to meet new people and being around great music. It was a nightlife of lights, music, and glamor that later became the center of my whole life, at least for a few years.

When I remember my high school years playing competitive softball, being a good athlete, being involved in the corporate life of the high school, playing the viola, having a lead role in musicals, and working on the magazine committee, it is with many positive memories. There was one creep of a teacher who, when I was seventeen and in my last year, wanted to photograph me "from birth to death." It was very weird indeed. I confided my concerns about him to another teacher, Mrs. Lovie, and she "sorted it out" swiftly and cleanly.

In addition to Mrs. Lovie, I had other really cool and helpful teachers during high school—the science teacher who looked like Michael Cole out of *Mod Squad*; Canadian Sam Peckinpaugh, my art teacher; the school headmistress, Mrs. Scott; my English teacher; and David Cox, my math teacher. I stayed in contact with many of them after I left high school. Dave came to my 21st coming-out birthday party in June 1978, and Mrs. Scott took me to lunch at one of Canberra's finest restaurants to celebrate my 21st. These were the influential and important people who impacted my life in such positive and nurturing ways, and many years later Dave even taught my stepson, Derek, and also my son, Nick, at the same high school.

Counterbalanced to any negatives I experienced were other happy memories. I was chosen in 1970 as one of only twelve to sing at the Australian War Memorial for Queen Elizabeth II, Prince Phillip, Prince Charles, and Princess Anne. I felt so special being a good enough singer to be presented formally to the Queen. Singing for her and Prince Phillip was the highlight of my school years, and one of the markers in my life that subsequently defined who I am and the values I hold dear. It's funny how I remember my first impressions of all of them—Lizzie so regal, gracious, and cherub-faced; Prince Phillip so tall, handsome, and strong-looking; Charles with such big ears and nose, but with nice eyes and a beautiful, deep voice; and Anne, huge teeth and looking a lot older than she actually was.

One home where we lived was on a dangerous intersection and very close to my high school. That home was where I learned to survive on intermittent sleep. I was icy cold in bed during wintertime. The heating system was just a briquette fire in the lounge room, and we never seemed to have enough briquettes to fire up. When we did, I would start them burning and, of course, get into trouble for burning too many to heat the house before mother came home that night. The heat never seemed to get to my bedroom at the back of the house. The house must not have been well insulated. In winter, every morning I would wake to find water on my windowsills and damp bedclothes. Summer and spring were my reprieves.

One weekend night, a motorcyclist had a very bad accident. He was hit by a car on that intersection. I remember being woken up to the sound of his moans. I was only about fourteen or fifteen but went outside to see what I could do to help. His helmet had come off, and he was bleeding. Someone across the road had called the police, but it seemed like ages until I decided this poor fellow needed a cup of tea. Grandma had always taught me that a cup of warm, sweet, and milky tea was good to help stop people going into shock. She was right, and years later when I actually dated that gorgeous young accident victim, he told me how good it felt to drink that cup of tea; to have someone by him who cared about him and kept him warm with a blanket. He was a stunning young man, and after we'd stopped dating, I always wondered if he'd found a nice woman to settle down.

It was during that time, 1971–1973, that I was starting to feel very insecure about myself and my life. I was doing the deportment thing, really involved in school activities, had a good circle of friends, never short of a job to go to, but I was under so much pressure. I suffered from bad headaches that time, bit my nails right down to the skin, and felt very insecure in my ability to do well at school. Years later at the thirty-year reunion, many of my old female friends came up to see how life had turned out for me. They recounted times when I would vomit uncontrollably before exams, and that I was always saying how if I didn't do well my mother would punish me. The pressure was ridiculous for someone who was working so hard to please, yet always seemed to come up short of other people's expectations.

In my second last year of high school, we moved from the red-brick, corner Ainslie home to a new home in a nonhousing commission part of Canberra, a suburb called Hawker. Hawker was the first suburb not to have government-subsidized housing in it—very posh, very affluent. But boy, what a trek to school! My after-school and weekend jobs became a real chore to get to given that I didn't have a car. Most of my income was spent on fares.

Other family had access to cars, but I was left to fend for myself on public transport. The home we moved to was the ultimate in luxury living to me in many respects—something quite strange to me for all the daggy places I had lived as a smaller child. The hardest part was I was still the chief cleaner, washing clothes, vacuuming, cooking, ironing, and even landscaping the dirt patches that would eventually become gardens. My mother refused to allow full heating of the house in the wintertime. I had the chore of firing up the heating systems wherever we lived. Mother always claimed that she couldn't afford the heating.

The Hawker home was double-story with three garages, living and bedrooms upstairs, and a downstairs flat. The flat had a separate entrance on the side of the house and also internal access to the garage. I couldn't, for the life of me, work out how my mother came to afford that place, until I found one of her government pay slips while vacuuming her bedroom one Saturday. She earned so much money each fortnight, and heaps of it was siphoned off to a savings account. The level of income and the home itself was completely contradictory to the way she spoke about her "hard life," and how she did not have enough money to pay for everything. She was always out somewhere, rarely home at night or on weekends, and always had political party things to go to. It just didn't compute. There were many political party activities held at that home by my mother that I knew to be immoral and illegal. All of the standards my grandma had taught me were being breached.

In the latter part of 1973, I asked my mother's permission to have the after-school musical party at this new home. There was no carpet on the floorboards, no heating, no drapes, and no gardens. The windows were still dirty from the builders having been there, but somehow I managed to pull together the whole cast, orchestra, and teachers from school to have a blast of a party at that house. Everyone brought his or her own food, drinks, and music. Grandma and Pa were there that night. Pa found couples smooching in back rooms and shooed them out into the light of the kitchen. It seemed like people were just everywhere, swarming all over the house. But there were no fights and nothing bad happened.

The next day we were all off on another event I had organized—the customary trip away to celebrate another successful Gilbert and Sullivan musical—to the ski fields in the Snowy Mountains. We all had a blast. I returned from that trip to the job of cleaning the house and found Pavlova and cake remnants everywhere. Someone shoved cigarette butts down into central heating floor vents—what a surprise to see how some people would treat a new home. And the stains on the floor—where on Earth did they come from?

My mind boggled at the thought of what people had gotten up to.

Chapter 5

From late 1973 and into 1974, I used to catch the bus to work traveling at very odd hours sometimes. As a consequence, I met a bus driver twelve years my senior. I was sixteen at the time, and he was twenty-eight. Because I was so mature for my age and experienced in work, we just hit it off. We spent a lot of time talking over the months leading to our first sexual encounter. Unbeknown to me at the time, he was married and his wife was pregnant with their first baby. We "dated" via bus trips, drives in his car, dinners at a local restaurant, followed by physical relations afterward in a motel room he had secretly booked. All the while, I had no idea of his marriage and other life. I always wondered why he would be interested in a young woman my age, someone still five years from being declared a legal adult—although I had reached the age of consent at sixteen.

One time he asked me to go away for the weekend with him to the coast. I asked my mother for her advice, and all she could say was, "You do what you think is best." That was little help. I agonized over the decision whether to go for what seemed like weeks, ultimately deciding no. I didn't go—something just didn't add up. With help from my friends, I started to investigate and uncover things that seemed to be hidden. Upon finding out he was married, coupled with the shock of the news of his unborn child, I quickly put a stop to the association.

The one good thing he did was teach me how to drive and park in tight places. For that I am grateful—he knew all the smart moves in cars. We met twice later in life, once in 1989, when I was married and he had twice divorced. He was really struggling to get his life together. Then again in about 2004, at a produce and craft market. He was with his third wife whom I had worked with in 1989. She saw me and must have said something to him. She motioned me over, and it was a shock to see this once-handsome man reduced to a shell. He seemed so far removed from the man I'd known. He did tell me he was sorry, and for that he regained my respect. My key lessons from knowing him are if someone drives dangerously in the car with you in it, you can bet your life they do not value your life. When a man squirms or refuses to answer direct questions or won't let you see where he lives, he is likely hiding more than you would even want to know. Follow your gut instinct when it comes to intimate relationships. If it doesn't feel right, and there is little or no explanation why, then get out. Saying a sincere sorry is the first step to righting a wrong. Sometimes one sorry is all that is needed to fix a major wrong or a series of wrongs.

In late 1973, at the ripe age of sixteen, I was in my last and busiest year at high school. I was also in my first senior management role and feeling a lot stronger about how well my life would track. Juggling school assignments, homework, exams, school, volunteer work, housework, and the demands of a management job that had me on the bus to work before 6:00 a.m. on a weekend and home after dark was certainly a hard time. Somehow I survived and grew more resilient as a result. I was the catering manager for a cruise-and-coach business that operated in Canberra and surrounding districts—coaches to here, there, and everywhere. I worked on two cruise boats that offered lunches, dinners, events, and afternoon and morning tea cruises around Lake Burley Griffin. My staff and direct reports ranged from retired navy captains, deckhands, and female catering staff. Despite the occasional bitchy catering assistant who couldn't cope with being supervised by someone so much younger, it was an amazing job. I eventually had to take the company owners to the labor tribunal for not paying me proper wages. The thing I remember the most fondly were the lovely captains who would call me up to the top deck after catering service was over and say, "Here you go, you've got the wheel." Letting me steer was against the rules as I learned some time later, but they let me guide the boat in between the pylons of the bridges that spanned the huge lake! They trusted and respected me. What a great job and life that was.

From 1973 through 1978, I also did professional modeling on the side—lots of TV ads, photoshoots, runway modeling, and charity events. I gained a diploma from one of only a handful of good modeling academies in the country at the time, Kimberley. Modeling wasn't something that was my life goal, and to a certain extent, I always felt that the 1970s were a time when women were cheapened by such activities. We were really just giant coat hangers for clothes or pretty faces to be ogled at.

I had a lot of fun during those years, but my portfolio and the many TV ads were the highlight for me. My close friend from school, Katie, did my portfolio for me when she was a photography student. Katie took what I still consider to be the most beautiful photos of me at the time. She was a natural, gifted photographer then and still is now.

During that period of modeling, I went to my agent's house one day. When she wasn't home, I ventured back to my car. Things were amiss next door; something funny was going on. I was one of a few people who entered the home of the elderly man who lived there, and instead of finding him alive and well, we found his corpse. The smell, the look—they stayed with me vividly for years. Now with just a memory of the overall event and without the smell lingering in my nose, I feel sorry that he died alone in his home without someone to be there at the end.

In 1975, as an offshoot of some of the runway modeling, I entered a major beauty contest in Canberra. As finalists, we stood on stage and listened as the judges read out the winner's name: Nola Jones. I was Nola and the other finalist was Naomi Jones. But my family's name was originally Jones—so was I still the winner? What a complete mix-up. By the time you could blink twice, they were apologizing to me and congratulating her. I was embarrassed and mortified all at the same time—we were live on national TV!

When I walked down the runway at the end and stepped off the stage to join the audience, men and women came from all directions. "We thought you should have won; you are much more beautiful. You look even more beautiful than in the still photos they showed on the screen," they said. I was grateful and warmed by their kindness, but it didn't help my feelings of humiliation and disappointment.

The only negative thing about beauty contests in those days was that society conditioned women to believe that if they didn't win, they weren't beautiful. I thought, *I'm not pretty enough.* I'd never considered myself a natural beauty, not like Elizabeth Taylor or Marilyn Monroe. I believe that true beauty comes from within, and if your soul is beautiful, then the outside will reflect that in one way or another—through your eyes, your smile, your manner, your voice. To be beautiful inside and out, which many people in my life insist I am, is a bonus. I don't look in the mirror and expect to look beautiful each day. But I do work on being the purest and best I can be at a soul level every day, and that is how I want my inner beauty to be expressed.

The highlight of my last year at high school in 1974 was the end-of-year cruise my mother paid for me to go on. I think it was her way of saying, "Well done." This was the first time she gave to me in a way that felt genuine.

That cruise was so much fun. I went with Katie, and we had a ball. There were some unhappy moments like being teased, and her pictures attest to my reaction. But 99 percent of the time, it was exciting and pure fun. Freedom had come to my life in a different kind of way.

Katie won the beauty contest during the cruise to New Zealand on the Russian cruise ship *Leonid Sobinov* and received a bottle of Russian champagne. In October 2012, when I met up with Katie for the first time in nearly thirty-eight years, I went to her home in the USA and met her husband. There at her house was that bottle of champagne. I said to her husband, Tony, "It'll probably be like a Sauterne by now," and sure enough, it was very rich but still drinkable. What a lovely surprise and a real treat to share that part of history with her. That trip was a memory I will treasure forever.

Katie didn't remember Nell and Dell, the rather overweight spinster sisters with whom we shared our cabin. They were hilarious to observe. Their big Bombay bloomers, which are huge, full-sized panties, would be hung on the clothesline from one side of the cabin to the other. Katie and I would always be getting back late from our nights out, always pretty sure of ourselves. We probably giggled a lot, too much for the sisters to cope with. What a contrast of cabin buddies.

I met some wonderful people on that cruise—the chef, stewards, and deckhands. I learned quite a few words of Russian, which I still remember. A couple of funny memories include when we went to breakfast one morning and what I thought was a glass of water on the table was actually vodka. I downed it, being thirsty and all, and became quite instantly intoxicated. My Pa had always warned me about vodka being the silent-but-deadly drink. I finally knew what he meant.

Another memory was when we visited Milford Sound. We had to get off the ship into our designated lifeboat for the trip over to the sides of the Sound. Milford Sound is still one of the most captivating places I have ever been. Every season came that day we were there; it snowed, it was hot, it was cloudy, and it smelt of fresh flowers and spring. When we got into our lifeboat and fastened our life vests, the motor wouldn't start. It was so funny! The deckhands in charge of the lifeboat were embarrassed, and even though I was concerned for our safety, we managed to row out to the middle of the water and take a closer look at the majesty of the rocks and waterfalls. It was a good thing we didn't have to abandon ship at any stage during that cruise!

Chapter 6

During that last year of high school, I had my heart set on studying to be a physiotherapist. I had been accepted into Melbourne University, but when it came time to leave, my mother worked and worked to convince me not to go. In hindsight, I realized she not only wanted to control my destiny, but also wanted to keep me around to do all the work in the home. I was devastated once again. As I was not yet a legal adult, she had the legal right to dictate my path. My dreams were destroyed.

During December, after I returned from the cruise, my mother pushed me to take up hospitality industry studies. I was only halfway interested, although I did love the feeling of the industry, being so people-focused and happy. I agreed to enroll in studies for a Hotel Management and Catering certificate, and subsequently studied and passed a variety of subjects during 1975 and 1976.

I had two years of the French chef's course. I learned everything there is to know about liquor and liquor service, from tapping kegs of beer to mixing and devising cocktails, to being a real sommelier. I learned so much about wine and spirits manufacture and production that my taste in wine is very refined. I learned how to prepare and serve food "silver service," how to prepare food at the table using a Guerdon cart, and then how to serve guests in the correct manner. I learned how to be a maître d' and a butcher—how to carve up hindquarters and forequarters of beef, a whole lamb, and a whole pig into correct portions and cuts. I learned how to make sausages and how to identify and produce food-poisoning bacteria in a controlled laboratory setting. The ease with which food can deteriorate was eye-opening. To this day I share food safety with everyone. I learned management techniques like estimating costs to determine prices for selling food and meals. I learned how to design and prepare lavish menus, and I learned the skills necessary to cater and cook for dozens of people with total ease.

As far as men in my life go, during 1975, I was in awe of a ballet dancer, a gorgeous young man. We became close, dated for a while, but were never intimate. He left to live in Melbourne; I was devastated. One young man my age I met in 1976 through some fellow college students was an interesting character. We were never in love or even emotionally close to any great extent, but we were a couple, and I enjoyed his company. We lived separately. Once, quite humorously, we engaged in partner swapping with another of our couple friends. This was my one and only heterosexual orgy with four people in the room participating. It was a hilarious experience, but I wouldn't ever expose myself to an orgy again. It just didn't seem right to be unfaithful to my own boyfriend with another man, even though he encouraged it.

During that year I also had a brief, live-out relationship with a former boss who had owned a restaurant I'd worked in. Once again, he was some fifteen or so years older than me. He seemed to know everything about life and treated me very well. He showered me with gifts, and we had a nice time. I always wondered if, in secret, he was married to someone. There were things that didn't add up, and he had possessions that seemed like the possessions of a couple. We spent a large amount of time at his place over the course of a few months. He taught me sexual boundaries that were very helpful from that point on.

I learned so much during those two years at college and in industry, and in the latter part of 1976, I won an executive management role at one of two international five-star hotels in the capital city of Canberra. I was only nineteen years old and had enormous responsibilities as the second in charge to the general manager and third in line to the top of the company.

My role with the hotel was a lot of shift work that I didn't really mind. The general manager worked Monday through Friday, and I had to cover those and other periods when he was away. There was a junior manager who worked small shifts to give me some time off, but I was there for every major event, wedding, function, conference, VIP visit, and most night service. It was a very busy role, but one that I loved.

Some of the real highlights of that time included being responsible for the well-being and comfort of VIP guests, government dignitaries, and visiting diplomats. Folks like Andrew Peacock, Australia's foreign minister at the time, was a frequent and regular guest. When I knew he was coming into town, I would arrange for housekeeping to prepare his room just the way he liked it. We prepared and locked off the sauna from other guests, and then I dined with him in the restaurant at his request. Andrew was a lovely, articulate, intelligent, and polite man. I went out of my way to make sure he was always happy with our service. Our conversations were always edifying and stimulating.

Then there was the band Dr. Hook that I really enjoyed. They came to Canberra on tour in 1976 and stayed at the hotel. I had the privilege to be on duty the day they arrived, and it was my job as manager to make sure they had everything they needed. Instead of delegating to housekeeping, I opted to iron their jeans for their concert in their suite, listening to them jamming several songs. Ray Sawyer was hysterically funny, cheeky, and just so lovable; Dennis Locorriere was ever so nice and such a gentleman with one of the most beautiful, husky voices in the world. Their music was spot-on perfect; they were all such gentlemen, so polite, so appreciative, so authentic, and so genuinely nice. They were some of the nicest people on this planet and just natural in front of me. Their energy was great, and they thought I was amazing for ironing their jeans.

Dennis sang a version of "When You're in Love with a Beautiful Woman," one of my favorite Dr. Hook hits. That day, I had a bird's-eye view of one of the greatest shows on Earth. Sometimes they would deliberately make jokes mid song, and then start back at the beginning. They laughed at and with one another and me. It just seemed to go on forever, that afternoon. If they only could have seen the smile on the inside of my heart. What a great chance to have shared that magical few hours with them, being a part of their lives for a nanosecond in time.

Spending many hours over many night shifts managing male guests and their requests for "escorts" (i.e., prostitutes) was also an eye-opener. The hotel had an old PBX switchboard—plug-in/plug-out wires going everywhere. In the middle of the night, certain guests, and you could usually pick on check-in which ones would ask, would phone down and ask to be connected to certain numbers. They must have thought the hotel switch staff were naïve. We had a list of all the local brothels and escort agencies—all illegal, of course.

We'd connect them through to the escort service, and usually within twenty to thirty minutes, some dressed-up female would walk through the front door looking like she'd just stepped off of a movie set. It was hilarious. At one-hour intervals on my 10:00 p.m. to 7:00 a.m. shift, I'd be walking the corridors of the hotel with the biggest bag of security keys in hand, looking for guests' indiscretions and security issues. At least once per shift, one or more of the following would happen: the escort would storm out of the hotel's front doors upset; a pair of nickers would appear in the hotel's swimming pool the next morning; guests would be locked outside their rooms, usually butt naked, by angry escorts; guests would phone down again within an hour of the last escort leaving and ask to be connected to a different number; guests would look as guilty as all heck when they checked out the next morning; and rooms would look like a bomb had been dropped inside. Of course the staff and I would be even more amused when regular guests would have us ring their "usual number." It opened my eyes to life in a way I never thought possible.

Being in such a high-profile industry and role, I got to attend many entertainment industry functions, meeting various artists who visited Canberra and VIP guests from overseas. The one meeting that left a lasting impression was when I was having a quiet afternoon glass of wine at one of the city's other fine hotels accompanied by a friend from work. Into the reception area walked a famous Australian band with their entourage of groupies. They literally took over the hotel lounge and became loud, obnoxious, rude, and abrasive within the hour. I left that hotel disgusted at their behavior but most importantly, disappointed that they felt they had the right to be so badly behaved. They exhibited arrogance and selfishness like I have never quite witnessed since. By comparison to real stars like Dr. Hook, they showed their true colors as redneck wannabes with no respect for anyone.

In the same year, 1976, I was deeply, emotionally connected to a fellow student who was Fijian. We were the best of friends but were never a couple. He later came to my twenty-first birthday party in 1978, and I still have a picture of us dancing and the gift he gave me. He was gentle, intelligent, funny, and deliberate. I'll always hold special, happy thoughts of him. I missed him for quite a few years after he'd returned to Fiji.

During the summer of 1976, I was in a live-out relationship with a young man twelve months younger than me. He lived down the road, and I'd met him through one of my college teachers when I used to babysit the teacher's three young boys. I became the "surfie" chick; he was very much into surfboards, and I was into suntanning.

We spent many weekends at the coast, but things started to become weird when the college teacher's wife, an insatiable sexaholic I came to find out, started to have an extra-marital affair with my young man. I couldn't stomach the thought of being around him after he'd slept with a next-door woman who was eighteen years older. That turn of events triggered the beginning of the end of the friendship with the teacher's family. That young man I dated ultimately died in a car crash just after my twenty-first birthday—such a shame.

By late 1976, I was frustrated with my career and unsure of my future. I was doing volunteer relief work and tutoring students at a local grade school. The experience was satisfying, but it was not my future career. The hotel role was a dead end; I could see that coming. I'd reached the highest level any woman was going to achieve due to gender barriers, and the actual job was not going to change. I bit the bullet and put feelers out for the next chapter in my career and life. Now was my chance at a new start away from Canberra and a new career doing something more challenging.

Over the next couple of months, I applied to join Officer Cadet School (OCS) in the Australian Women's Army Corps (WAC). Women were segregated from men, and the WAC OCS was supposedly looking for capable women to lead. I was one of many hundreds of applicants, and finally after psychiatric interviews, tests, and interrogation-style questioning, I was chosen as one of the final twelve to visit WAC headquarters in Sydney. That day I'll never forget. The senior officer of the WAC, a colonel, was on my right-hand side at lunch. She had a moustache and looked butch. Her 2-I-C was on my left and looked equally masculine.

The Regimental Sergeant Major (RSM) who sat opposite me at lunch yelled at the finalists for what seemed like all day. The lunch was as much our chance to make a final decision as it was theirs. I looked down at my painted fingernails. I looked at the RSM and at the officers on either side of me. I thought about nightclubs and dancing, fun and laughter, and I thought to myself, *Outta here me!* There was no way I was joining the WAC. I didn't want to end up a dyke, ugly, sporting a moustache or anything similar.

One of my "what do I dos" involved auditioning for the National Institute of Dramatic Art, the famous NIDA, in Sydney. I was only half-motivated, so I rehearsed my lines on the way down in the airplane and didn't prepare an impromptu piece. I figured if it was meant to be impromptu, then that's exactly what it would be. The audition didn't result in my being offered a place, although they liked my singing and some of the scripted pieces. Acting wasn't my dream then—maybe that is why I didn't get chosen. It was fun, and I still went on to do some singing and acting later in life. I had a go at being a dental assistant, but it was not for me. Finally I sat the entrance exam for the Australian Public Service, ultimately winning a base-grade clerk position based in Sydney. The job was my chance to move away from Canberra.

Chapter 7

Late in January 1977, I moved to live in a motel at Five Dock for a few months while I settled into Sydney life. I'd bought my first car by then, a 1957 Morris Major Elite, using a $500 cash advance from my new bankcard. I was a bus ride to work at Pitt Street in the heart of the city, and I'd enrolled in a bachelor of science degree at the NSW Institute of Technology. The six months there were mixed with family visits with aunts, uncles, and cousins. I also spent time dating, studying, working, and knitting.

The physical, on-off, live-out relationship with a second cousin of mine was very unusual. How had we gotten together in the first place? We enjoyed each other's company, and for him, the sex must have been good. The lesson I learned from that is best not to dally with relatives.

Knitting was my escape from sad thoughts; it focused my energies on positive, forward outcomes. I provided support to an aunt when her mother died, and that was the first time I started to accept and verbalize that my mother's and my relationship was not healthy. In May of 1977, my mother encouraged me to send a Mother's Day card to that aunt. That hurt so much. My mother was pushing me away, emotionally. I've come to see that since, but at the time, it was so hurtful.

My aunt and I were close, and quite naturally, as my mother pushed me away, I became even closer to her. I distinctly remember saying to her, "My mother is toxic to me—I don't know why; it just doesn't feel right being around her." My aunt was upset to hear me say that, but she came to understand a little more over the last forty years. My aunt and I have remained close, although we see each other rarely these days.

During that time in Sydney, through my aunt and her husband, my blood uncle, I came to meet my father for the first time since childhood. Dad had been estranged from me since I was a toddler. The relationship with my mother and grandparents had become so tense he felt it best to bow out of my life. The night I met with him was a bit strange. I was seeing him through my mother's eyes and lies. Dad gave me a beautiful solid-black opal gemstone that he had mined himself at Lightning Ridge. I had the opal set into a dress ring and have kept it close through all these years. Dad really was like a stranger to me, and I felt that having contact with him would betray my mother. I ceased to write to him after I left Sydney.

The public service job I had in Sydney was boring beyond belief. Imagine sitting in a small room with four rows of desks in it—the one you're in and three rows in front of you. Everyone is facing forward, and all that can be seen from the back row is a sea of backs. I accepted a base-grade clerk's role and along with two others at that level, we processed fortnightly payrolls for staff working at three veteran rehabilitation hospitals in Sydney. As each pay cycle ended and people were paid, the new pay cycle began. It was a monotonous cycle whereby we, in the back row and the lowest paid, would calculate everyone's pay. We'd pass our paperwork and computations to the person directly in front who was the next level up in grade two or three. They would then check our calculations, and likewise pass the checked paperwork forward to the next row to the higher-paid grade-four clerks. After the grade fours had triple checked the calculations, then the pay sheets were handed to the finance section to arrange payment. That was the cycle. If something was queried or found wrong, then the paperwork would get handed back down the line again, to the base-grade clerk to do it all over again from scratch. Nightmare!

Lest I forget the two weeks just before I took up the base-grade clerk's job I had to wait for an opening in the veterans' department, so the public service offered me a tea lady's job at the Maritime Services Board at Circular Quay in Sydney. It was located down near the Domain where many of the city's homeless and derelict would sleep at night. It was a very seedy and undesirable location to work.

A few short weeks earlier, I had been managing a five-star hotel with teams of staff all over the hotel all doing their thing, humming along quite nicely, and dining with VIPs and diplomats. A few weeks later, I was wheeling a trolley with hot-water urns, cookies, coffee, teabags, hot chocolate, cakes, and greasy fried foods, serving rude and arrogant public servants who had nothing better to do than complain about their day, their pay, or their significant other.

That was my first experience as the "leader on the shop floor," seeing just how badly people can be treated based on the level of the job they hold or the capability they're presumed to have. No mind was paid to the past life of the person wheeling the trolley, just a cursory flip of the hand and snide comment if the tea trolley didn't serve them what they wanted. My time there was such a learning experience, and it taught me a lot about what not to teach my staff and others during my second climb to the top of my profession.

I was never one to be sexist or prejudiced in any way, and I couldn't understand such rudeness. I was also aware that people hold very different standards in the workplace, like the Nazi head chef claiming he'd cut off the protrusions of any non-blonde, blue-eyed person in his kitchen. Not even then would I do anything other than manage with pleasantness and diplomacy. In his case, his employment was actually terminated when he threatened more violence and also fancied me as his means to procreate a supreme race of blonde, blue-eyed citizens.

To manage the chronic boredom of the public service job, I went to the local university and studied for my degree. I loved to study and really thrived in that environment. I also applied for a computer programmer's job, which meant I had to move back to Canberra again if I won it. Intellectual stimulation was vital for me to maintain any level of normality and happiness in life.

I won the job, moved back to Canberra, ceased my studies in Sydney, found an apartment to live in, and enrolled part-time in a new bachelor of arts degree, studying computing and law. My government job meant that I could get time off work to travel to university lectures and tutorials. I was so busy but happy, nonetheless.

I had a programmer's job running subroutine changes via punch cards onto magnetic tape and then into the main computer. I had to wait two to three days for program check turnaround, fix the subroutines, or write new ones. The cycle started again. The job was boring beyond comprehension. There was no people interaction, and worst of all, every time I looked up from my desk, I saw the back of the head of my supervisor, a grade-four clerk. In seven months, not once did she say, "Hello," "Good morning," or "How are you?".

By January 1978, I'd had a gutful of the public service mentality, bureaucracy, lack of people-focus, and slowness of decision-making. I resigned and decided to work in a restaurant/nightclub at night and on weekends while studying full-time during the week at university. It was good for me to be out and about again. With my contacts in the hospitality industry, I quickly got some part-time work for extra money and, during one of those shifts, I met Tina Turner who had come into the restaurant I worked in for a relax after performing at the city's central theatre. Tina was stressed looking in those days but still a brilliant performer and was so sociable and nice to everyone. She was such a lovely natured lady from what I could see.

Chapter 8

During that year, I also had a few brief relationships. One was with an ex-college teacher-chef. We met by accident and just decided to get physical, a bit of a fantasy fulfilled on my part. My lesson from that was all about older guys talking themselves up but not necessarily being the best.

I met a young man who had been burned badly as a child. We met at a nightclub, and it took a long time for me to connect with him on a mental and emotional level. We dated for a couple of months early in the year, but his extensive burns were his barrier to real intimacy—something he wanted and I did my best to understand and help him with. After we'd split, he invited himself to my twenty-first birthday party, an act not favorably taken by anyone. To this day, I have never quite worked out how he came to be so arrogant. I learned that giving a man time to come to terms with his feelings and express himself will either give a result that you want or result in your torture, if you care about him as a human being.

For a while, I dated a marketing executive who had an MG sports car that we used to take for long drives into the country. He was a nice guy, but an old grade school nonfriend we mutually knew was jealous of me. We were always marred by her attempts to split us up. We lived in our own homes but spent loads of time at his place. The relationship lasted about four months and was lots of fun. I didn't learn any real lessons from him.

After moving back to Canberra, I also bought a new car through my first personal loan. I was impressed to have achieved a loan so young to buy a new Nissan 120Y four-door sedan. Soon after the purchase, I took my seventeen-year-old younger cousin, Michelle, on a road trip to South Australia. I was not yet a legal adult myself, and still her parents allowed me to take her along. It became a holiday to remember. We stayed west of Adelaide first and attended a superb open-air concert. That was where I saw Billy Thorpe and the Aztecs the one and only time.

In Adelaide, we had drinks at a five-star hotel the night Reg Livermore was playing impromptu piano in the lounge. Reg was then one of Australia's most-gifted entertainers, famous for his versatility and range of capabilities. We visited beaches, driving onto the actual sand of the beach, which was a real novelty for me. We also met several sexy men along the way. We travelled to the Barossa Valley wineries and spent one night in a caravan park that we thought would be quiet and relaxing. However, in the middle of the night, a goods train thundered past just three feet from the back window above my bed! We enjoyed German pastries from the locals in Barossa and tasted some of the best table and fortified wine Australia had to offer.

But then Michelle became quite ill with low blood pressure. She had a low resting-heart rate anyway, but something triggered for her, and she started to look like a ghost and became slow and incoherent. I had her in my car and headed back to Melbourne, a twelve-hour nonstop drive. We arrived at her parents' holiday home at Ocean Grove around 5:00 a.m. on Sunday and scared the living daylights out of her siblings who woke to the fright of us knocking at the windows to be let in. There was no harm, and Michelle was given the medical OK. The trip became a topic of discussion and laughter for many years to come.

For a short time in 1978, I lived in my own apartment. But with money getting a bit tight because I was working only part-time, I had to return to rent the flat below my mother's house. All went well for a few weeks until I met a new young man, who was actually a heroin addict. He was pure charm and had dashing good looks, but he was as deceitful and conniving as they come. My life started to unravel. Drug addicts have a way of introducing bad into your life.

We lived together at the Hawker house after my twenty-first birthday. Little did I know every time he went to the bathroom and locked the door, he was secretly shooting up. I was never naïve, not ever in my life, but he sure had me fooled. That's what addicts, particularly hard-core smack addicts, do. They use every trick in the book to hide their habit. That young man caused me a huge amount of emotional and financial grief at the time, not the least finding out he was a heroin addict of very high standing in the criminal underworld. He took my new car out once and, as a consequence of not paying for some drugs, some of his associates bashed the car to bits.

My mother's health at forty-seven was already failing. She had high blood pressure, was always fatigued, suffered from anxiety attacks, never ate well, was overweight, and physically lazy. I was being the mother to my own mother again. One night she was midway through a hypertension attack and came downstairs to our flat in the early morning hours. As a consequence of her symptoms, I took her to the hospital promptly. The doctors advised her about what to change, but she pretty much ignored their advice. She seemed to always know better than they did. She refused the medication and the suggested dietary changes. It was a very frustrating and upsetting time for me as I tried to convince her to look after herself better.

Social life for me was full and interesting, though. I had loads of friends and held many parties and dinner parties, but sustaining only part-time work hours with intensive full-time university studies was becoming financially impossible. In the spring of 1978, I applied for and won a brand-new permanent role in the computer industry. The industry would come to have a life-changing and positive effect on me. For the next eleven years, I enjoyed everything about it—computers, education, sales, marketing, travel, and people.

I joined an international South-African owned company in their Canberra office, where I provided technical and educational support to a range of government and private-sector clients. I supported the sales force by doing technical demonstrations, preparing tender responses, and with their technical queries. My efforts won me a promotion to the Melbourne office. The world opened up for me there.

I followed my instinct and got the heroin addict out of my life the second I discovered his extracurricular activities. I also found out that he was sexually promiscuous. But not before he nearly caused me to lose that new computer job that I'd started in September. I was tracking him down all over Sydney to find out what was going on. He was into prostitutes and became a drug dealer. My absence for a few days, unexpectedly, caused a major rift with one of my female colleagues who had led what I called an "easy" life. She had to fill the gap in my absence and was mortified at having to actually work for once.

There were some really sound and memorable relationship lessons I learned during that time with the addict. Most of all is that dashing and charming on the surface can be a nightmare underneath. Beware the ones who won't let you in the bathroom, even when you've been living together for ages, get the shakes and can't seem to settle until they "go visit a friend," suddenly disappear for days or weeks on end, or have other personal hygiene and bathroom issues surface for no logical reason.

I came to see how his life turned out sometime around 1986. I flew into Canberra from a business trip away. I had company-paid cab vouchers, and I went to line up at the taxicab queue. There he was disoriented, unshaven, skinny, and unkempt. He was the cab attendant. I said hello and introduced myself; he had no idea who I was. The years of taking drugs, psychotic episodes, and drug-induced comas had taken their toll. As I left in the cab, I remember thinking, *So that's how your life turned out? Glad I didn't hook up with you.* I think these days people say, "You dodged a bullet with that one." I sure did with him.

Montage of me from 9 months to 21 years of age

Childhood friend Louise (bottom row, 3rd from left) and I (second top row, 4th from left)

On my tricycle at Grandma's and Pa's, Sydney c. 1958

On the waterfront at Sussex Inlet c. 1958

At Sussex Inlet c. 1964

In the backyard at Young Street Concord

Presenting my first-ever black fish, Sussex Inlet c. 1968

One of my favorite pictures, in full character as Pitti-Sing

Pitti-Sing, in pink in the middle, one of the three little maids from school, *The Mikado* 1973

Grandma and Pa at a family wedding in the early 1970s

The *Leonid Sobinov* "bouncer" decided I needed to be removed; what a hysterical night of fun 1974

Rowing Pa's dingy up Sussex Inlet, May 1974

Me on the left, with Kate, visiting the NZ Bay of Islands during our cruise, December 1974

Portfolio pictures taken by Kate 1975

Cousin Michelle (left), me (right), and a friend of Michelle's (middle), Ocean Grove VIC 1979

With my Celica 1979

At my 21st birthday party; Pa is the one on my right wearing spectacles

Bicycle tour with Jesse around Rottnest Island, WA, stopping to feed the quokkas, May 1980

The Peace Angel

"*New York, New York*" opening number, yours truly on front right, May 1981

With the other models during the opening number, May 1981

Dancing to George Benson, the sleepwear segment, with Greg

With Greg in our chic attire, May 1981—the hat I had on was the softest cashmere

Greg and I in front for rehearsal time for the Myer Charity Fashion Extravaganza, May 1981

One of many mementos from the event, May 1981

At Sydney International being farewelled by Myer and Westfield colleagues, May 1981

With Jesse's family dog Snooky, June 1981

Bonnie gave me her jacket to remember her by, December 1982

Grandma's and Pa's serene home at Sussex Inlet NSW

Chapter 9

Based in Melbourne, I had an absolute ball working to create and install a range of computing solutions across industry and government. I enjoyed training people on computers and was even headhunted by IBM but turned them down. Melbourne afforded me a rich and full social life ranging from jazz music Sundays at Box Hill Pub, to disco at the Melbourne Hilton, to frequenting places where, I found out later, the rich and yuppie set hung out. My network of friends was large and growing.

Melbourne life for almost fifteen months was nothing short of a blast. We still had drive-in movies, and I'd catch local Collingwood football games at the MCG. I'd dine out at the cute little Spanish restaurant near Fitzroy Tennis Club, imagining myself learning flamenco one day. I even got to drink white wine from a goat skin one night—no spills and total fun.

Many weekends were spent enjoying the sun and fun of Ocean Grove. It was there I'd spent a long summer school holiday when I was fifteen. Years later in 1991, when I was on holiday there with my then eight-year-old son, I took him to Ocean Grove Surf Club. There on the wall was a picture of me, taken when I was around eighteen, sitting on the front of the club's surf racing boat. I had no idea the picture of me in a bikini adorning the bow of the boat would be hung on the wall for the world to see. I was a little embarrassed but got over it soon enough.

In Melbourne I progressed from living in a rented one-bedroom flat to a three-bedroom home with a pool. My mother made a few visits and insisted that she, wanting to do something different than the public service, should come to Melbourne and have us go into business together as a word processing bureau. Once again, I felt her wanting to live her life through me. She saw me succeeding and wanted to join in.

My love interests were few in 1979; they included a relationship with the CEO of the company where I worked. He treated me very well, and I thought he was a marvelous person. Sex was adventurous and most enjoyable, and I could have lived life with him quite easily. It became complicated when he told me he'd had a physical relationship with a woman in my office the year before, but he said that it was over. She obviously didn't think it was over or was keen to get reacquainted.

I remember one visit to Melbourne when he stayed with me on Sunday night. We dressed for work that Monday morning, and I dropped him off at the corner so he could walk in the main entrance while I parked my car in the underground car park. As I entered the office area, we caught each other's eye— his look was reassuring. I felt safe that we were safe. But then, on she came, all over him like a rash and flirting beyond belief. He looked awkward, and unfortunately, what we had fizzled quite badly after that. I don't think he cheated on me, but she obviously had no idea I was the new woman in his life and had been for quite a few months. I enjoyed some lovely trips to Sydney for weekends. He only took me to the best restaurants, and we cruised on Sydney Harbor on his or someone else's yacht. It was a great time and a pity it ended the way it did.

After the CEO experience, I was hurting. I had never felt a sense of true love as an adult like I always wanted to feel. When the opportunity presented itself, I had a physical and emotional bonding with a visiting branch manager. I was in punish-the-CEO mode within myself and really had become disillusioned by men—at all of twenty-one years old. I didn't find him attractive and definitely didn't love him, but I did like him. The interesting knock-on effect was I heard the CEO transferred him to Perth to banish him for doing something wrong in the company. And low and behold, I was offered a new role in Perth.

My mother's pressuring me to go into business with her coincided with the new role in Perth. I'd been in dialogue with Wordplex, the mother company to the one I worked for, and they were hinting about my working in the USA one day. In Melbourne I'd bought a gorgeous little yellow two-door Celica with mag wheels and leather upholstery. It was my most favorite car for many years and it too was shipped off to Perth.

Chapter 10

I flew across to the West in very early 1980, not knowing what was yet to come. However, the next big moment came. I had to work in the same office again with this manager I'd slept with, and he was my new boss! Had he fixed that situation to serve his purpose? I'll never know. But my mistake came back to bite me—he wanted more.

I managed to twist and dodge him until he got the message soon after I arrived, but then I started to receive the worst workplace treatment. My key lesson was: never get physical with someone who could one day become your boss. It is never a good outcome, especially if you reject him later. You will come out the worse if you're not in the position of power.

The job in Perth was a step back professionally. I went from a fast-paced, high-profile, and large office in Melbourne to small-city Perth on the other side of the country. People greeted me with, "You know what WA stands for don't you?" "No," was my reply. "Wait awhile," was their answer.

Perth was only two hours behind in time but a decade behind in experience, technology, thinking, and there was no inspirational culture in the city at all. Perth has lovely beaches, more sunshine than anywhere else on Earth, magnificent scenery, and vastness of land like you'd only see in parts of Africa. But it was just so quiet and lifeless.

That, of course, didn't stop me. I decided I would put life into Perth even if it killed me. I sang at a cute little jazz bar in South Fremantle on weekends, and I played tennis with upcoming journalist Terry Willesee, brother of the famous Aussie journalist Mike, at City Beach Tennis Club. I went out finding and buying antique furniture on weekends, and I danced everywhere I could find that was nice.

I was having quite a nice life across the country from my family but something was missing. One day I decided to go on a famous Swan River wine-and-cheese cruise, and that is where I met him—Jesse. He was tall, dark-haired, handsome, and intriguing. I thought he was sexy, funny, with soft eyes and a beautiful physique. He spoke in the accent I have come to love—Texan. There he was, the kind of man Louise Devine and I had described to each other over and over again sitting in that bathtub at Young Street—a real masculine man.

From the wine cruise, Jesse and I, along with his offshore work buddies, went to the Perth Hilton that night for some disco dancing. What an amazing, sexy dancer he was. Everything about him was perfect—his looks, his hands, his humor, his smell, the feel and color of his skin, his accent, his manner, and his politeness. Life was bringing me the gift I'd always wanted.

Jesse worked off-shore and was gone for weeks at a time. That didn't really bother me. I just got on with my work in the meantime. When he was coming back onshore, he'd fly in from far away (the North-West Shelf), but he and his friends always seemed to have drunk a lot during the flight. That in itself wasn't an issue, but I always wondered why so much? I held parties at my home for him and our friends, and he would stay with me whenever he was onshore. We travelled around to all sorts of places together when I wasn't working. Rottnest Island was a super day trip. Jesse, being used to flat-bottomed boats, could handle the wave motion on the boat that takes you across to Rottnest. It took me longer to get my sea legs. We rode bicycles around the island and fed the quokkas.

During one of Jesse's breaks, we decided to do the Perth-to-Sydney cross-country drive by car, crossing the Nullarbor Plain in my Celica. On that trip, Jesse met some of my family, including my mother, in Sydney. My mother was always sort-of jealous or wary of my relationships she knew about, and at one point during the visit in Sydney, she pulled me aside and said, "He's got money!"

My first thought was, *What? What has that got to do with anything?* I started to strongly back away from her and her manipulative comments. Pa, her father, had always brought his children up to believe that having money or acquiring financial wealth and freedom was wrong. In any respect, my mother's comment put me right off her, and I immediately took Jesse's side. He wasn't showering me with gifts; he was just him. He was a good man and good to me, and I loved that about him.

By the time we got back to Perth a fortnight later, I knew that I had fallen head over heels in love with him. He was just so easy to be with. He went back to his boat, and a few weeks later, I arranged a ship-to-shore phone call. I had no idea that a ship's phone is usually on loud speaker, so when I said, "I miss my handsome Texan," he seemed to become very embarrassed. He quietly whispered that all the guys on the boat could hear what I'd said. I wasn't embarrassed for me, but I was for him. I felt really bad that I had exposed him and my feelings that way, even though I thought we were speaking in private.

Not long after that, Jesse moved on with his company to the South China Sea. He was headed back to the USA eventually. I don't recall the farewell event when he left, though we did agree that if at any time I was in the USA, I would be welcome to visit with him. I thought that was nice and hoped I would see him again.

His absence left a hole in my life that was palpable. It took me many months to accept he had a life away from me, and that we had essentially split up. But this man was not replaceable, not at all. He had left a mark on my soul that I couldn't explain, even to myself. I don't remember ever telling him I loved him even though I had those feelings.

We really did have a great time there, in my view, and his leaving was a major part of my losing interest in staying so far away on the West Coast. In mid-winter 1980, I decided to resign from my role in ICT and move back east. The hint of a possible US job was looking very exciting, so I sold my beautiful Celica and many pieces of furniture in anticipation of the move to the USA. I packed up the home I was renting in Pangbourne Street Wembley and arranged a removalist. My household things went off to Sydney to be stored with friends there temporarily, and I left for the Gold Coast in Queensland to help my mother set up a small restaurant/café at Mermaid Beach. Mother had no idea where to start, and I'd been in the industry after all. This was her escape from the public service she said.

Chapter 11

Initially I agreed to work for nothing to help her out, but after a month of no money to go anywhere or do anything and with a loan to pay, I felt like I was being well and truly ripped off. I negotiated, with a whole lot of effort, $100 per week. I worked around fifty to sixty hours each week in the café and doing the books. That wage was daylight robbery, below the minimum wage, disrespectful to the senior skills and experience I had, and I considered it to be slave labor. I was helping her out at a difficult time in her life, even though she was blatantly getting all she could out of me for little or nothing in return.

Around December 1980, I became friends with a gorgeous-natured gay guy. He became my best mate and the buffer between me and straight men. I was beginning to shy away from men out of self-protection and also because Jesse was on my mind so much. He encouraged me to still date, given that Jesse and I had officially split and there was no guarantee I would ever see him again. I did look, had one brief physical encounter with a lovely, romantic Italian-Spaniard who was visiting on a tourist's visa, but never had any real relationship during that few months up north in Queensland.

Once summer became full on and soon after the New Year celebrations in 1981, I became pretty jack-full of my situation working in the café. I saw no future in Queensland and started to make moves to leave for Sydney. A new life was calling, and my mother was thinking of selling up to make a profit and buy an investment unit on the Gold Coast. So much for my less-than-minimum-wage help to her. I'd engaged a singing teacher while I was there, and he asked me to sing in the Murwillumbah Eisteddfod that year. But opera singing wasn't my gig. My voice was good enough, but it wasn't my dream. As much as I loved theatre and performing, he wanted it more than me.

My arrival in Sydney early 1981 meant one of two things—a new life there or a move to the USA when everything got sorted through. Being up in the air about whether the USA was going to happen was disconcerting, but I didn't let it overlay my life. I had my multi-entry visa in my passport and had pretty much given up hope by the time the important calls started to come from Thousand Oaks and Culver City, California. I now had an offer from Wordplex to move to New York to provide marketing support to their branch manager. The future was looking really wonderful. I didn't feel like I had any real familial connection in Australia anymore, except Grandma and Pa who were quite elderly at that stage, and the USA was a whole new world of unknowns and excitement.

Between February and May, while I was filling my days in a managerial role for Myer Ltd, mixing in modeling and fashion circles again, having a wow of a time managing a whole range of fun activities and meeting some famous and fabulous people, I was also planning for the future.

Life was never dull, and the most memorable highlights in my career from that time in Sydney included interviewing both John Newcombe, the acclaimed tennis star, and author Judith Krantz. Meeting Judith was a turning point for me in pushing me down the path of being an author. I knew what I wanted to write, but didn't have the proper vehicle to make it happen at that time.

Running a big fashion extravaganza for Myer Ltd and the Society for Crippled Children, specifically to raise funds for our entrant in the Mrs. NSW Quest, a major fund-raising event for the charity, was a fabulous and fun time. As a consequence of running that event and the amount of effort that went into fund-raising, the charity offered me the top fund-raising manager's role. If I hadn't been going to New York City, I would certainly have considered taking that job.

Every part of that extravaganza was fun—creating the choreography, choosing the models, planning clothes and the music, working with the art department on the stage backdrops, and all the logistics. From start to finish, it was a pleasure to be involved, and I still have the thank you card from the entrant Lyn and other mementos of the event.

The one and only time I lived on a cliff top was there in Sydney in 1981. It was on the easternmost point of Cronulla, a southern suburb of Sydney laced with some of the best beaches in the country. The salt spray was constant, but I felt like I was breathing God's clean and moist air every time I went onto the rusted balcony of my rented flat to look across the rocks and out to sea. That flat was such a peaceful and pretty place to live.

It was there in Sydney that I was offered a vintage white Jag by an old ICT industry colleague. I very nearly bought it just as a keepsake but always wondered how I would keep up the repairs cost as it got older. I was headed to the USA too—I couldn't have both. Little did I know then that in 2012, my company would come to buy an XF luxury white Jag. It's funny how things turn out.

My possessions were already down to a minimum when I moved to Sydney. By the time I'd committed to leave for the USA, garage sales were on the go every weekend. Reducing my possessions from a four-bedroom house full of stuff in Perth down to just a few boxes and suitcases of what I called important essentials wasn't hard to do. That letting go of unsentimental possessions is always a refreshing and de-cluttering way to simplify life at the best of times. I felt free again to go where I wanted when the time was right.

At the time of my plan to leave Australia for good in 1981, my mother seemed to come alive with helpfulness. She went halves with me on a new carry-on bag to supplement my one and only suitcase. I chose carefully every critical thing I would need to start my new life. Photographs, clothes, a gift for Jesse, and keepsakes were very important to me. The household and precious items like silverware, twenty-first birthday gifts, and crystal could come later, and they did arrive thanks to my mother freighting them over. Moving to the USA had become a certainty by late March with my flight out booked for May, but prior to that, there were a solid couple of months where I didn't know where my life was headed. Everything was so up in the air and out of my control about the USA and what might be with Jesse if I went there.

One of the most difficult things for me to navigate in life at that time was an event brought about by my dating a star football player for a short time. Our relationship was fine; we dated for a while, but it all ended badly when he had me over to his group house one night and there were two of his rugby friends, waiting for me to arrive too. A frightening and unpleasant experience ensued; however, I managed to extricate myself. They took photos of me with my boyfriend without my knowledge, photos I found on my way out of the house that night. I had to threaten police action so they let me leave in peace and made them promise to stay right away from me.

That short-lived relationship with the footballer left a very bad taste in my mouth and a strong distrust of men in general. I remember being terrified at one point not knowing whether to speak up that night and obviously risk being bashed or worse. All the guys were paralytic drunk, maybe even stoned, and really had no control of themselves. But they were strong, and I was not nearly as physically strong then as I am now. The power difference was huge. I took those photos with me to the USA so that they stayed safely in my hands. I had no idea what might have happened had the photos stayed in their reach.

On the upside, I developed a friendship with one of the models who donated his time for the Extravaganza event. He was a very sweet and handsome man about ten to twelve years older than me. We were close, but we didn't have a relationship. He took me to some wonderful high-profile glamour-life events run by Sydney's biggest entertainment industry giants. Life with him was certainly going to be glitz and glamour and beautiful people, but the USA was calling. He came to the airport to see me off and said he'd be there for me if I ever needed him. One of the other models once told me she knew he had strong feelings for me—I had no idea how much he felt until I was leaving. My relationship with him helped me restore my faith in men to a degree.

In late May of 1981, I flew to the USA to live. It was my first time on a plane leaving the country, and it was my first time to the USA. I was greeted by the company's senior executive at Los Angeles International Airport. After a few days of work-related activities in Los Angeles and a change in plans as to where I would be working, I went off to Texas to spend a fortnight with Jesse before starting my new job.

On arrival at Houston airport, I was greeted by what seemed like a whole bunch of his friends, along with Jesse. We piled into someone's car, and I sat in the back seat with a couple of others. No sooner had I begun to gather my feelings about seeing Jesse again, when someone reaches to the back seat with this scoop-looking thing with white powder in it. "Welcome to Texas!" I was told, followed by huge laughter—it was a cocaine-snorting device. My body had been so clean and unpolluted by drugs. They were something I associated with grief, loss, crime, disappointment, and destruction. How could this be that this was life in Texas? But I went along with it. I didn't want to question things. I just went with the flow. I had no idea what was or wasn't legal, but found out soon enough.

Those couple of weeks in Texas were chock full of family activities and visits, combined birthday celebrations at his mother's home in Austin, a party at his stepbrother's house, touring and cruising around to wonderful restaurants and nightclubs, and I met his mom, stepdad, daddy, stepmom, his half brother, many other family members, and his friends. The trip just seemed to get better and better with every day. I felt so welcomed, warmly and genuinely. I felt a sense of real belonging I have never felt with any group of people in my life, except for how I felt around some of my family in Australia, and particularly how I felt around Grandma and Pa.

It was also different then. I saw Jesse on his home soil, a different man in many ways to the one I remembered in Australia only a short time ago. I saw how he and his mother related, which was good for the most part, but I sensed something was amiss.

Jesse always had things on the go with things happening, always fixin' to be somewhere, or planning something for us to do. The one thing I'll never forget is how I felt safe with him. No matter where we were or who we were with, I felt like he would be there to protect me. I'd never felt like that around any other man and never have since I was with him. A whirlwind effect had begun for me and lots of feelings for him reemerged.

We had reconnected physically, and it was a disappointment when I had to go back to Los Angeles after such an amazing and happy two weeks. In the middle of my holiday visit with Jesse, my official letter of offer for my new job arrived. Rather than sign it and send it back, I held onto the letter and waited until I'd gone back to Los Angeles.

On first arrival in Los Angeles, I'd encountered the nightmare, sleazy new boss. When I went back to Los Angeles in mid-June, given I'd had a bit of experience with the ulterior motives of bosses and men before, I became wary when the new California boss started officially changing the plan. He wanted me working for him in Culver City, managing Southeast Asia marketing operations under his higher direction and living in his trailer home.

The opportunity of the dream job in NYC disappeared before my eyes. It was difficult to change to suit the culture of the USA, but I was promoted to a senior international role only days after coming to the country. I felt it was becoming too much, with the seedy off-the-cuff comments from the new boss from Culver City as well. Loud alarm bells went off in me from left, right, and center. All I could think of was, *Jesse, help!*

I spent a couple of sleepless nights alone in a hotel room, mulling over what to do. I rang and spoke to Jesse and did my best, without disclosing my very real fears and safety concerns, to work out what to do next. I decided to decline the job in Los Angeles, forego gaining a Green Card through them, and came to Texas to make a start there.

Chapter 12

I sensed that decision to come back to Texas wasn't in Jesse's plan, but he was being supportive as a friend at least. I guess he just figured that I would work elsewhere in the USA and eventually get my Green Card. I never really knew where I stood with him or what he really wanted from or with me. We were just together, without questions and without reasons. I went back to Texas and was warmly welcomed once again by his family and him. Jesse left to work in the Gulf of Mexico, and, in the interim, I moved into his mom's rental home. Within a week or so, I had found work. The doors were opening, and I kept going with the flow.

After a few months, Jesse's half-brother's girlfriend bought the rental home, and I was starting to feel like I needed to move out. Jesse and I decided to move into an apartment elsewhere in Austin; his mom gave us some dining room furniture and bed to get us started. Jesse bought a new lounge suite, and I bought household items to get us underway. His mom was being really helpful. By that stage, I had had the most important two boxes of my life's treasures sent over by my mother. All the special sentimental things like silverware, crystal, and linens were there with us in that apartment.

Around early fall of 1981, I was comfortable in my work with the nicest boss I could ever wish for, Al from Annandale Engineering. My work colleagues were the sweetest, most polite men and really funny to be around. I loved my life in Texas. In October, Jesse took me on a weekend holiday to Mexico. I'd cashed in my return ticket and was working toward getting my Green Card. I had income and was feeling safe and secure.

I felt comfortable with Jesse just the way he was, though I didn't understand why he would get so angry sometimes. After having borrowed his stepmom's car for a few months, and her not being happy about it, we were out one day driving around with Jesse's half-brother. Something triggered a huge anger response in him. He banged his fist into the dashboard of her car that day and cracked the dash molding. I just froze. I remember when Jesse got out of the car really mad about something, and I just looked at his stepbrother with tears in my eyes. He said to me, "It's OK; he'll be OK." I had no idea how to deal with that level of anger from someone who had always been so calm and considerate. I didn't know if it was me that had made him mad. All my life I was the one blamed. If someone got mad, it was my fault; if someone didn't like something, it was my fault. I just figured Jesse's anger was all my fault.

For a while, I was quite cautious, careful about what I said, and how I said it. I felt like I was walking on eggshells a lot of the time around him. I thought I had left a life of anger and criticism behind me. But what I found was the more I tried to please Jesse and be accommodating, the more he disregarded me, acted critical, and dismissed what I wanted. At one point, when we first moved into the apartment, I was down on my hands and knees scrubbing out the kitchen cupboards to clean them for our things to be put away. He was sitting at the kitchen table with one of his friends, a cocaine and pill addict and a pretty ordinary character, from all observations. Jesse all of a sudden came out with, "Damn, look at that bitch work!" Bitch? Since when do you call a hard-working, caring, and nice person a bitch? I worked out over time that that was just the way some young men spoke to their women in Texas. Unbelievably disrespectful and uncalled for, but I'd made my choice. I had to learn to live with that kind of comment. I guessed that was a Texan's way of romancing.

Despite the differences in our views about some things and his angry outbursts around me, I loved him unconditionally. For all the things I would love to have changed about him, I didn't attempt to. I knew another side of him that was caring, protective, considerate, passionate, loving, and decent. I accepted him for who he was on his home soil, and figured if he was going to become a better person and more like he had been in Australia, then it would be by his choice and not by my design.

Through Christmas 1981, we had a life that was tracking in a way that gave me considerable comfort in many respects. After the trip to Mexico in October, he mentioned in an offhanded way one day that his friends had asked him if we were going to get engaged. I listened, not really knowing if he was hinting to me, but I don't recall we ever really discussed it. During his stepbrother's Halloween party in Houston, I began to feel very insecure following something he'd said. He obviously didn't read me very well and accused me of thinking and feeling something that I simply didn't. In 2010, I saw a photo taken at that party, and I was stooped over like the weight of the world was on my shoulders. I looked like I was cowering to protect myself. That was a shock to see all those years later. What I had been feeling from time to time in 1981, when Jesse criticized me, was manifesting in my body language so clearly.

At Thanksgiving with his family and in our own apartment, Jesse was making off-the-cuff comments again. "People think we're married. . . . It's like we're married." We never sat down and really discussed it. I was confused, unsure of his intentions, and unsure whether to ask him outright. Yet in every other respect, our relationship, which was the most important love of my life, was perfect beyond anything I could imagine. This relationship was so different and real compared to what I had experienced before. But, while I was quite fearful of rocking the boat and asking for explanations, on the flipside, I was constantly feeling like I had to stand my ground when his family and friends would start changing things to suit themselves.

My closest girlfriend there once said to me, "You're so different when he's not around." I knew exactly what she meant. I felt like my own person when Jesse was away—not walking on eggshells, able to shine and do things that I liked doing too, feeling no pressure to please him first and do things the way he always wanted, and putting my own needs last. I had lost myself in amongst the us.

By Christmastime, I had been quite sick a couple of times and unsure what my body was doing—loads of reproductive system pain and abnormal signs and symptoms were starting. I was not hearing from my mother at all, despite months of my letters going to Australia. I felt like I was being shut out from all angles.

That Christmas we went to Tyler to visit Jesse's mom and stepdad. Jesse and I had been living together in Australia and Texas, and yet despite our being adults and that history, Jesse's mom wouldn't allow us to sleep in the same room together. I was distraught, and I was missing my grandparents in Australia whom I saw almost every Christmas. I felt like no one was listening to how I felt. They weren't, not really. Jesse, to the extent that he understood what I was going through, explained it as just his mom's rules. Maybe there was a religious undertone, although I'd never gotten that feeling before around her. I just felt there was more at work than she was really willing to let on. For example, months before while Jesse was offshore, she arranged for me, her, and her husband and stepson to all go out dancing. It would have taken a blind person not to realize I was in love with Jesse; however, she insisted we go out when the stepbrother was in town. For many years, I kept all the photos of my life in Texas. After I'd forgiven her under hypnosis in 2002, I tore up that photo she took of the stepbrother and me dancing, along with many others that reflected the hurtful aspects of my life with Jesse and her influence. I kept only the pictures that represented the happy times when someone else wasn't controlling my outcomes.

There was quite a lot about life in Texas that was foreign to me. I had spent my childhood under severe constraints. Here in Texas, money was no object to most people. The economy was strong and jobs were available. It had taken me a while to adjust to the new culture and lifestyle.

But I have to say, Jesse's mom gave me more as a surrogate mom during that first eight months in Texas than my own mother had for most of my life. She made a beautiful combined birthday cake for Jesse and me in early June, welcomed me in her home, and treated me as more family than visitor. She made sure I was comfortable and had everything I needed to make my stay in her home pleasant. I was included in family events held at their home, like croquet, and it was so much fun. When I used to look at all the photos of those times after I returned to Australia, I could see how happy and content I was most of the time. It really was a fabulous time in my life, despite the occasional negatives.

The first four months of 1982 were the real turning point period for me. Those months were an awful, heart-wrenching period of my life that took me over twenty years to recover from and forgive.

In January, Jesse was away at one point when I became very ill at home in our apartment. I remember that winter it had snowed heavily in Austin for the first time in years—a record snowfall. I was in so much agony with what seemed like a twisted something in my abdomen. I called an ambulance. I was taken to hospital and operated on for a ruptured ovarian cyst. That was the diagnosis I had waited to hear. For years I had loads of abdominal pain I couldn't explain during my early twenties.

Jesse's mom came to help out. She did provide really wonderful support to me while I was in the hospital, but it was when I returned home that I got a huge shock. She had changed things around in my own home. This was my and Jesse's home, not just Jesse's. And it was certainly not her home to substitute ornaments, buy new things, and generally fix up the way she liked it. I felt she should have left it the way we liked it. I was speechless and feeling very confronted by her intrusive style. Maybe she meant well, but she sure did overstep the mark of privacy and respect for others.

At another point late in February of 1982, I realized my visitor's visa had expired. Having been forced to change jobs due to ill health and needing to earn more, I was frantically working to source a stronger work sponsor for my Green Card and had not paid attention to the dates. Jesse and some other friends referred to me as a "saltback," and it was so hurtful. The circumstances had played out such that I was backed into a corner, with one job ending and my new employer deliberately putting my Green Card application to the side, saying they didn't have grounds to sponsor me.

All of this occurred after Jesse had written a personal check to me for $500 back in 1981—the deposit toward my

Green Card application in Texas. I couldn't work it out. *Did he want me around or not? Whose side was he on?*

Through March, things were OK for Jesse and me except for the Green Card hassles. I was feeling much better health-wise, better than I had in many years. The doctors in January had explained the consequences of having a long-standing ovarian cyst and how that plays havoc with the hormonal system and ovulation. They assured me I didn't need contraception for at least six months. That was a welcome relief, as I had been on the pill for several years, and that had not helped my overall health one bit. But sometime late January or into February, I became pregnant with Jesse's child.

By late March, I had an idea something was different, and a blood test at the doctor's confirmed it. I was at least six to eight weeks by that stage. Jesse was offshore at the time. I spent a while getting my head around the fact that I was pregnant when the doctor's had given me a verbal guarantee that I couldn't. I went to visit a close friend to tell her the news. She was over the moon happy for me; she knew how much I loved Jesse and was so happy about me being pregnant. I was too. I'd seen her give birth in February to a beautiful boy, and I was feeling very clucky around her baby.

I rang Jesse using ship-to-shore radio connection and asked to speak to him in private. I told him the news, and his immediate and heart-wrenching reaction was fear and anger. He said, "We're not getting married." Marriage wasn't even on my mind. I felt betrayed by his anger. After we hung up, that conversation and the shock of what he said was made worse by the fact that on previous occasions he had made noises about engagement, marriage, and other people's comments to him about a future life. I figured if he'd truly known he wanted to marry me at some stage, I doubt he would have reacted that way. The more I asked him to talk about it with me, the more he shut me down, closed off, and wouldn't respond to my communication. I was lost, shut out, and abandoned in the worst kind of way by a man that I admired, loved, respected, and with whom I wanted to build a life. The baby, to me, was like God's gift to us, and he didn't appear to want it!

For about a week, I sat alone going over all the things I had done in previous months. I had gone to look at houses for sale near where friends lived during September through December of 1981. I worked hard to gain my residency legally and worked hard at a commission-only job where my employer didn't pay me the commissions I was due, time and time again. It was a God-awful mess. Suddenly the family I had come to love and see as my own and feel a part of in so many ways I couldn't turn to. Jesse had rejected me and the baby, and I thought they would as well. I had absolutely no idea what to do, or who to reach out to other than two girlfriends.

During a brief conversation, Jesse did indicate that he expected me to fix the situation. By not helping me talk through the potential solutions, I sat alone thinking through what would likely play out. If he threw me out, I could become homeless, and without my employer paying my commissions, I probably would not be able to fend for myself or the baby. I could stay pregnant and return to Australia where my mother would certainly take over my life, the baby, and everything else, including Jesse's parental rights. I could maybe find another job, but my Green Card would be so much harder to get as a pregnant woman alone in the country. It's only been in the last few years or so that I've realized if he had at least helped me out until the baby was born, I could have stayed in the USA and found a job to support myself and the baby. That would have been a far better outcome than the one that came to be for the baby and my new life there.

By early April, without any support from anyone other than my two girlfriends, I really felt the pressure building. The silence from Jesse was a killer. I had no idea what he was thinking, wanting, or feeling. All I could think of was finding a solution and quick. He was due to come home, and I needed to get things sorted. I was terrified to ask his stepmom or mom what to do. I believed Jesse would surely have seen that as going behind his back. I remember thinking at that point, *Well, you've got me over a barrel, don't you?* The barrel was, in my mind, a gun pointed at me by his family. They wanted this baby gone, no matter what.

I went to a clinic in Austin and had my first of two consultations. At the clinic, the termination procedure was explained to me—a twisted wire device would be inserted inside me to expand the cervix against Mother Nature's natural force to keep it closed. I felt sick as I left that first appointment. I remember really struggling to get through the next fortnight, going to work and not getting paid. If Jesse hadn't left me blank checks as a backup if I needed during the time he was offshore, I would never have gotten through that fortnight.

At the end of the fortnight, just before I was due to go back to the clinic, I finally got paid enough commission to pay for the procedure. My best friend was coming to the clinic with me that day, April 28, 1982. I have no memory of the exact events of the day leading up to the clinic visit, but I do remember feeling like I was being pushed hard down a path that I didn't want to go down. Never in my life had I ever felt so powerless to change the course of events.

My heart was racing by the time I got into the procedure room. I was helped up onto a gurney covered in a white sheet. My cervix had been aching so badly for those last couple of weeks, and I felt sick most of the time. I would cramp up and not be able to walk. I was a mess. A year or so later when I went into the final labor with my son in Australia, I remember thinking back to April 28 and the aching that was taking over my body. In Texas, I was essentially in labor without the contractions for two whole weeks.

I remember that I cried and cringed back with the worst emotional pain I had ever felt the whole time the doctor did what he had to do. The doctor and nurses asked me a few times if I was OK before they started. Did I still want to do this? I remember not being able to speak. I must have looked like a deer in the headlights. I was stunned, speechless, and helpless. Although more vaguely now than in earlier years, I remember the enormous force with which that baby was reefed from my body. I felt like my whole uterus was coming out. My girlfriend was waiting outside for me. She was just there, supporting me quietly, waiting.

Chapter 13

After the procedure, my friend took me to her house and got me completely stoned smoking marijuana. I know it helped me to separate myself from the emotional pain I was in, and for that, she was a godsend. I could be safely off with the fairies, resting at her home until I was ready to face the reality of what had happened. The doctors had explained that they had no guarantees what damage might have been done to my reproductive system. They believed that within the first trimester the risks were lower. After the procedure, I was having what seemed like a normal period, and I took certain precautions to prevent infection or hemorrhaging.

Somehow, with my girlfriend's help, I got through that day. When I got home, the apartment seemed like a surreal and cold place. I'd left there pregnant and come back without my baby in my body. It was extremely hard to manage my emotions at that time. I could feel myself strongly withdrawing and could do nothing about it. I know I went quiet and struggled to socialize with friends. I gave myself the worst mental time by punishing myself with negative thoughts.

A few days later, I went to another friend's place to attend a party. Jesse was coming back from the Gulf that day. He arrived at their home, and we didn't really speak much. We went upstairs to one of the guest bedrooms for a more private reunion. We made love that day, even though I was still in post-delivery, body-healing mode. I never did work out why he wanted to make love after all that had transpired. I was totally and completely confused by his reaction to me, his gentleness with me, and his unspoken support for me.

We returned home to our apartment that night, and after he unpacked his gear, we sat on the couch that faced the fireplace. That spot was my favorite spot with him. I was on his right-hand side, and he silently moved his left hand across to my abdomen. He looked at me with such a depth of emotion in his eyes. If I could have died and gone to Heaven, it would have helped ease the pain that shot into my heart. I thought, *Why, Jesse? If you regret this now, why didn't you say something before it was too late? Why?* My mind was full of questions all over again. My heart was breaking all over again.

Not long after that, another bomb was dropped. Jesse told me that after he'd come off the boat, just before he left Florida to come back home, he had been intimate with a girl he met at some club. I was stunned. I remember staying pretty calm and asking him why. His reply was truthful as always: "She was just there; I don't know why." At that point, I knew what we had, all the dreams I had for a beautiful life with him, was over. How could he do that, especially when I had just terminated a pregnancy because there was no other option known or available to me?

I'd given him what he wanted—the situation was fixed. Was the pregnancy and what I'd been through all too much for him? I felt inadequate and pointless to his existence. Like so many women, I continued to blame and punish myself.

May of 1982 was a hard month for me despite some happy times. Pictures show that we were still socializing with friends and had them over to our apartment. I drank heavily to numb the pain, began smoking again, and even passed out drunk at a dance hall one night. I had no emotional energy to pick myself up. It felt like Jesse had me at arm's length. I could feel myself slipping from the happy, vibrant, and positive person I'd always been to becoming an empty shell full of guilt. I was in punish-myself mode.

Jesse had taught me how to shoot a .45 Ruger and pump-action shotgun. He taught me all about gun safety, but one night around that time we must have had some sort of argument. I went into the bedroom and locked the door. I really wanted to be alone, to sort things out in my head and heart, but he read me wrong and started yelling at me to unlock the door. What was he thinking? That I was going to hurt myself with the Ruger? That event turned into a major standoff and yelling match.

Coupled with that episode of misunderstanding and high emotion, we went to a pool party soon after that where a number of his family was present. One of his cousins made a deliberate and unwelcome pass at me, and I rejected him but stayed quiet about it. What did the cousin do in retaliation for the rejection? He told Jesse I'd come onto him. For the life of me, and I've seen this over and over in my life, when a woman rejects a man's advances, the man, bruised ego in hand, will make out that it was the woman coming onto him. I've never quite understood why men can't just own up and say, "That woman didn't fancy me, I read her wrong, or I'm not her type."

What was worst of all was that Jesse never once questioned his cousin's motives. It must have seemed to him all my fault and doing. I objected but was ignored. What was crystal clear to me then was that the cousin was fixing to make trouble. He was a manipulative piece of work. I could see it, but Jesse couldn't. Jesse's loyalty to me was being tested by the universe. I know that now in hindsight, and he didn't pass the test.

Shortly after that, Jesse and I agreed to part ways. We'd both had enough; I know I had. Perhaps getting pregnant was seen as a deliberate act on my part rather than the pure, unplanned event that it was. God allowed the pregnancy in the first place; an element of divine intervention had to have existed.

The timing of our parting was synchronous with much emotional turmoil in our lives. I unknowingly was suffering from post-traumatic stress, and a lot of the time between the end of April and the end of May, I felt that both of us would be better off if I were dead. At one point, I couldn't see anything positive coming of the future; I felt like I'd lost all control of my life. I was alone, and Jesse was away a lot. Ringing a girlfriend was my way of reaching out to talk, and she was there. She helped me realize that staying focused on the future and walking forward was good. I never told her I had thought of suicide, but I'm sure she knew it had crossed my mind at some point that night. I was so unhappy and withdrawn that night. I just couldn't find a way to end the hurt and the guilt I felt about the baby and to make things right with Jesse.

Jesse was gone back offshore by his birthday in early June. Around the time of my 25th birthday in June, before I moved out of the apartment we shared, some friends invited me on a camping trip, bringing a friend of theirs along as well. Things were OK by and large as we all knew one another. I felt relatively comfortable, until the tent sleeping arrangements became obvious. I was to sleep in the same tent as their friend. No way. I was mortified and for a number of reasons. I remember making excuses at the time, suggesting that I would be more comfortable sleeping outside under the stars. I didn't sleep very much that weekend because I had one eye open. The thought of sleeping with another man was abhorrent to me. My sentiment towards Jesse had either been misunderstood or ignored. I was still coming to terms with everything that had happened. It was an awful time, but, of course, I didn't really show that on the outside to many people. I kept so much inside, which is why the inner bomb just kept ticking.

I had my 25th birthday in our apartment, and then I moved away to San Antonio to share an apartment with another girlfriend. She was so supportive, but with my visa having expired and without a job and little money in the bank, I lived off two jelly donuts a day for two weeks. I lost what seemed like a whole bunch of weight, and I was really suffering health- and happiness-wise. At one stage, out of desperation to make a change, I even rang the immigration department and suggested I should be deported. They laughed at me, explained that they were not going to deport me, and suggested I leave the country of my own accord. Despite being frustrating, their advice turned out to be a better outcome, and I subsequently returned to Australia.

I returned by borrowing the airfare from my mother. It was the last thing in the world I wanted to do, but I had no other options available. I already had the phrase "saltback" running over and over in my head, I had little prospect of earning enough money to live, and I was without the man I loved. Life there seemed pointless. I was simply surviving and not living. Most of my household possessions were still at the apartment with Jesse. We'd split and were still on speaking terms, but the loose ends had not been tidied up.

Once I had made arrangements for my flight to Sydney, I rang him and asked if I could stay at the old apartment and gather some of my things to take back. He agreed. I only have a few clear memories of that time. We made love the night before I left on August 7, but I also slept on the couch for a while that night.

The next day going to the airport, Jesse and I didn't speak much. He was good to take me to the airport and see me off. He did not show any feelings the way I hoped would happen, and he did not ask me to reconsider and stay. Over and over in my head I kept thinking, *He doesn't want you here, just go.* My heart was breaking again, and I could never tell him how I felt. I don't remember ever telling him then or ever before that time, "I love you." I'd always been too afraid of his reaction. I was too overwhelmed to do any more than go through the motions of leaving and manage the logistics. It was like being in auto-pilot mode.

I quietly got on the plane with no big emotional farewell scene. We'd always gotten on quite well and loud emotional outbursts and good-byes were certainly not the norm for us in either Australia or in Texas. My heart was well and truly up in my throat like a heavy weight choking me. I was at the point of no return, and for the whole flight from Austin to El Paso I thought, *I want to get off and go back. I don't want to leave. Should I get off and go back? Will he be mad or happy to see me? I don't want to do this. I want to stay in Texas.* I cried and cried. Everyone on that plane must have wondered what the heck was going on.

My layover at LAX was long, and I know I walked around the airport in a real daze. I sat down for hours on the bench seats just looking at people walk by, staring blankly at magazines and books I'd bought. It was a surreal experience.

A sad end to what was once a fabulous fun time of exploring, joy, and surprise. For a fleeting moment, Jesse seemed like he wanted our baby. We had such fun times in both countries. Under the right circumstances, we were the best of buddies and got along so well. He was my best friend and the only man

I had ever felt 100 percent safe with. He really was the greatest and truest love of my life.

When I reflect back to those times in Texas, there are so many positive memories. There were immensely enjoyable and unmatchable experiences like learning how to dance two-step and polka with Jesse. He was a sensitive and attentive dancer, and, in my view, we moved like poetry in motion after the first few lessons were out of the way. We even got to two-step at Gruene Hall when they were making a movie there. I remember Jesse pulling me in real close with his hand in the small of my back, making sure we looked just right for the cameras on every turn. I rode a mechanical bull at a kicker joint in Austin one night. It was fun but painful! I never rode again; once was enough.

Another time I stepped into a hotel elevator and came face-to-face and toe-to-toe with Dolly Parton and Burt Reynolds who were in Texas filming *Best Little Whorehouse in Texas*. Jesse and I were in the same hotel attending a huge wedding of some friends of ours. I was skipping between floors attempting to keep up with the after-wedding celebrations happening on what seemed like every floor of the hotel. Jesse was ahead of me by at least one or two floors, and there they were, the most gorgeous woman with the biggest boobs and the highest high heels I'd ever seen, standing on the right of one of Hollywood's sexiest men.

I worked at Dobie Mall in Austin for a few months and that kept me well and truly in amongst the UT set. The nightlife of 6th Street and Congress Avenue was fabulous, and

I even attended Willie Nelson's impromptu jam sessions in the middle of the working week. Willie would fly into town in his helicopter and then just park it by the Colorado River—free concerts for the public to enjoy. There was no place like Austin for things like that to happen spontaneously.

Jesse and I visited so many barbeque joints, Oktoberfest, and chili cook-offs. I came to love chicken-fried steak, fried onion rings, and Sunday morning breakfast at Luby's cafeteria. Dancing two-step with Jesse and listening to live music was probably the best nurturing of my soul at that time. One of my favorite kicker joints was the San Antonio Rose just down the road from where we lived. It closed down sometime in the 1980s. There were good and bad honky-tonks, but the San Antonio Rose was one of the best.

Going to the James Family Reunion in Alto in summer 1981 was an eyeopener. I met so many of Jesse's family, it was hard to remember the names. Not long after that I learned of Jesse's Cherokee heritage—his grandmother Mammy was full blood as I recall, which would make Jesse one-quarter Cherokee. The appearance of the Cherokee is hard to describe—strikingly handsome, finely chiseled bone structure, cherub cheeks, full lips, and rich-toned skin color. Some looks that Jesse would give took my breath away at times, unbeknown to him. He is such a stunning and handsome man.

Texas and Australia are similar in many ways. They both have beautiful landscapes, friendly people, and wide-open spaces. It was relatively easy to adjust in that respect. Jesse did make sure that since I'd chosen to live in Texas, I needed to dress the right way and learn how to shoot. He bought me a beautiful pair of Dan Post lizard-skin boots. I bought western shirts, new jeans, a new western belt, and got used to wearing T-shirts a lot of the time. The way I dressed in Australia in business attire, nightclub outfits, stiletto shoes, and beach attire would soon become a memory. My accent even changed. After working for Al at Annandale Engineering, it was only a few weeks before our customers would say, "What?" when I said good morning or afternoon with my non-Texas accent. I soon dropped the fairly English way of speaking and developed a twang as authentic as most Texans born and bred.

Jesse taught me to shoot his Ruger .45 pistol and a pump-action shotgun. It was great fun! He taught me gun safety, first and foremost. We went out hunting for quail, duck, and deer quite a few times, as well as target shooting. I wasn't into the killing aspects so much as the outdoors part and the fun and excitement of something new and different each time. His grandparents—Mammy and Pappy—had a place in East Texas that was so beautiful and the scenery so breathtaking. I couldn't help but love every trip we took up there. That was where I learned about deer blinds and hunting in the deathly cold of winter. Even though the picture is long gone, I remember the old yellowed and rusty tractor that was in Pappy's backyard. I still have Mammy's recipe for Shrimp Paella in my recipe box—she was so generous, sharing famous family recipes with me. She was a fine, down-home country cook.

Our hunting spoils were often cooked at home in our smoker. We made quail barbequed to perfection even though some of the shot was still inside the bodies. Every bite we'd have to spit out some shot in between chews! Deer chili was always a hit too. Jesse taught me the correct way to tone up a chili—once the basic deer chili mix is made, sprinkle a bit of red chili powder or some finely chopped jalapeños into the mix and add a drizzle of beer. After that step, just let it boil, then repeat as often as required—a sprinkle of red chili, a drizzle of beer—until the flavor is perfect and the heat just right.

The winter I spent in Texas was one of the coldest on record at that time and the first time such a deep snow had fallen in many years. I loved it. Seeing my first White Christmas and seeing the way America celebrated Christmas was a learning experience too. I also got to see the importance of Thanksgiving for families and learned all the different public holidays and what they meant to Americans and their history. It made me never want to leave.

There are a few key lessons for me that stuck out from all the other experiences of our relationship: fear and silence can do way more harm to others than to yourself when you're going through a hard time. Don't ever allow anyone to force you to do something you don't want to do. Take time to think through life-changing decisions. I made the biggest mistake of my life ending our baby's life. Matters of the heart can tear your world apart for a while, but if you stay calm and patient, things have a way of healing. Respect that when a love ends, no matter what someone in that relationship might say, they need time to come to terms with their feelings and any sense of loss.

Chapter 14

My flight from Los Angeles to Sydney was equally as upsetting as the first leg from Austin to Los Angeles. I felt worse the further I got from Texas. What was I going back to—the same of what I'd left?

The only thing I could think of to keep me from going under was that I would get to see my grandparents soon, and I could get a job to get back on my feet financially. I wanted to stay in Sydney with my grandma, but she was too fragile and old. She lived in a retirement village. I wanted so much to be around her and live with her. I was twenty-five years old and felt vulnerable all over again.

I landed in Sydney on August 7, 1982. Upon arrival, I remember going straight to my grandmother's place. By then, Pa had gone into a nursing home and was suffering from severe Parkinson's disease and atherosclerosis. Grandma was alone at her retirement village home. Despite one of my not-so-nice cousins making a rude remark about my Texas twang, Grandma accepted me as a changed person. Being around her was just so easy. I didn't want to leave Sydney where she was and go to Canberra again. I loathed Canberra for its clique mentality, boring lifestyle, and no nightlife. It wasn't Texas. I had to make the most of a bad situation.

I returned to Canberra with my mother after a couple of days of seeing family in Sydney. My mother, the control tyrant, had found me a job in the ICT industry. I could pay her back the money I'd borrowed for my air ticket and start to sort out a financial situation she had actually created during my absence. I enjoyed my new job; it offered me intellectual stimulation. Within a week of starting that job, I met Bill, the man who eventually became my husband.

Bill was only a month past separating from his wife after she left, and he seemed like a man looking to be saved. I was in a vacuum with my own feelings. I lived surrounded by packed boxes lining the walls of my mother's one and only guest room in her small flat in Canberra's suburbs. I was feeling so empty. I missed Jesse more than words could explain, and I looked at photos every day and night wishing myself back there. I brought a ring of his back from Texas with me so I always had him close by. When I missed him, I'd get out that ring and just hold it. But I felt myself pulling back emotionally every time a sad memory would come to mind. After about a month, something just changed in me. It was like a switch had been flipped, and I woke up one morning thinking, *Well, Nola, you've got yourself into this mess. You have no one to blame but yourself, so get on with it. Get on with life.*

I did everything I could to press Jesse and our life in Texas to the back of my mind. I knew in my heart the love for him was deep, but he was so far away and nothing I could do would change that. I really had no idea how to let go of my depth of feeling for him. I let my heart love Jesse, but knew I had to open myself up to other possibilities. The only person who I thought I could care for, feel needed by, bring happiness to, and help support through a hard time was Bill. I wasn't thinking about what I needed; it was all about what I could do for a man. I was completely and totally on the rebound, and I knew I did not love Bill in any way. It was almost like I wanted to hurt myself. I was still smoking heavily at that time, having started smoking again in late April. I hurt myself deeply by rebounding from Jesse to Bill, and by doing so, I hurt a lot of other people too over time.

It took nearly three months before I agreed to go out to his property that he still owned with his estranged wife. Bill and his two adolescent children lived in a tin shed sitting on a remote, twenty-plus-acre plot of land, about a forty-five minute drive from anything like civilization. I felt like I was going to be the one to make right the wrong I felt his wife had made. I believed I was strong enough, caring enough, loving enough, and giving enough. I put every effort I could into making things better for them, and by mid-November 1982, I had moved out of my mother's place to live in the tin shed with Bill and his kids. Mother was paid back and I wanted out, but she did everything she could to stop me from leaving. It was the same struggle all over again. She'd whine about this and that and made it seem as if I was abandoning her. I couldn't stand her intense emotional manipulation.

The tin shed was a tin double garage that was converted to living quarters with an outdoor tin garden shed made into a bath/wash room. There was no shower until I moved there and insisted on some improvements and only a bucket for a toilet—very primitive and undesirable living conditions. I was strong enough to tolerate it, and I made the shed seem homely. I shot many snakes during that time living in the shed, and I learned that scorpions are more prevalent in Australia than in Texas.

Bill was totally focused on his children and mainly his sick daughter, Toni, who suffered from leukemia. He hadn't been good at providing the right food for them; the fridge was always bare. With my love of food and being a chef in the past, they all seemed quite happy with the new living arrangement. However, there was zero privacy when the children were there, which was every day except for every second weekend when they visited their mother.

I knew, even at that early stage, that I was only going to be in Bill's life for a period. I never really knew how long or little that time would be, and I saw him as someone who could potentially father a child for me. But deep down, I also knew that if I became pregnant, then I would commit to staying with Bill for my child's sake. I didn't want any future child to grow up like I did without a father around.

By December 1982, I felt like I was already or about to become pregnant. Around Christmastime, I remember going to bed and subsequently slept for four whole days. I know in my heart that was God's way to ensure I would keep my newly conceived baby. I awoke to find Bill sitting by my bed. He told me he had not left my side the whole time. I don't know if that's true or not; he used to lie all the time, so who knows? He said he thought I'd gotten sick like Toni and was upset at the thought of losing me. It was then I realized he had feelings for me in a way that I couldn't reciprocate. I had come to care about him as a person but was never in love or ever considered him a real friend. We just went from being work colleagues to being a full-blown family unit all within a few short months.

Pretty soon after confirming I was pregnant, the horrible morning sickness started. I had intense nausea, headaches, and was unbelievably tired all the time. It was awful. I couldn't work; I slept nearly all day. I was given some very heavy-duty drugs that gave me a few short weeks of reprieve from the morning sickness symptoms. A few months later in either April or May, I went into early labor. Early labor wasn't good, but the morning sickness subsided, which was a huge relief.

By February 1983, Toni was back in hospital having various tests. She had come out of remission around that time, and was in and out of the hospital in Sydney. Her mother and father travelled back and forth working out what to do. While Bill always told me to stay away from the hospital, my mother wanted to be a part of that life. She wanted to become the step grandmother, but the timing was wrong, and she didn't appreciate being told to stay put by Bill. She always had some remedy, some magical vitamin or mineral supplement that she said would fix Toni. I kept shaking my head on Bill's behalf.

At that time, Bill's estranged wife was pretty ticked off that I had made the tin-shed residence so homely and nice. She would drive out and drop wheelies in the dirt with her car, scream, and get angry. Her anger was getting way too much for me. With little support from Bill in the manner I needed, I was ready to leave despite my desire to have a baby with a father present in his or her life.

By late February, instead of leaving alone, Bill and I both left the acreage and moved into Canberra to a rental home. We lived there until six months after Nick, our son, was born. The acreage went up for sale to ensure property settlement happened between Bill and his first wife straight away. Bill and I got engaged in March, which was nice for our friends and work colleagues to be a part of. Bill filed for divorce from his ex-wife officially, which meant that his decree absolute would come by October when we planned to marry. Nick was due to be born on August 30, 1983. I decided I'd find a way of working out the baby-naming aspects so that my son had his father's name. I changed my name from Hennessy to Bill's surname; therefore, our marriage certificate shows two people of the same surname getting married.

Meeting and choosing to get engaged to Bill meant that I had to find a way to keep Jesse with me and not upset Bill in the process. When I gave Jesse's ring to Bill to wear in early 1983, I told him a lie about where it had come from, and for the next five years Bill wore it. I had Jesse with me in full view; I felt comforted that a small part of him would always be with me.

I know Bill knew I thought about Jesse—I still had photos. I was staying in contact with Jesse's family and my girlfriends. But the ring disappeared, like a lot of things from my time in Texas—keepsakes, mementos, and pictures. Things just seemed to go missing or Bill would whine until I got things out of sight or gave things to other people. When I think back to that time, I was phoning Jesse's stepbrother to have long chats when Bill wasn't home or was outside doing things. I stayed connected with Jesse's stepmom and daddy, often writing long letters and sending cards. I was writing to some of my girlfriends—staying in touch—hoping and praying that I would get to go back.

By contrast, not once did I ask Bill to get rid of the photos he had of his first wife and their life together. I always wondered why he wanted it one way for him and a different way for me. I asked him why, but I never got a reply. I have since come to know his manner was all about him having supreme levels of control and manipulating a situation to suit himself.

Chapter 15

The year 1983 was an interesting and tumultuous one. I know I underwent a millennia of life journeys in just nine months. In all that time, not once did I sit and wallow in self-pity or reflect on the negative aspects of life before that. The past seemed so far in the past. The terminal illness of a child is such a daunting period in any parent's life, and on top of that, I had enough on my plate to deal with apart from my own pregnancy. I did my best to stay focused on the positive, and I'm sure without that mind-set, I could surely have sunk into darkness.

In February, when the move into the rental home into Canberra suburbia happened, I was amidst the debilitating morning sickness. Bill was away with Toni in Sydney with her leukemia treatments and preparing for a bone-marrow transplant, her last option for survival. Bill's divorce was underway. By most people's standards, one of these would have been enough to bring you down, but there was more.

During those early months, Bill and I also spent a lot of time with Pa. He rarely got to get out of the nursing home and

Bill, with a background in aged care, was able to lift him without aids. I visited Pa many times during my pregnancy, but he had me confused with my mother. He'd call me his daughter.

One day, when I found him in a terrible state on a porta-toilet, unattended and wet all over, I managed to get him back into bed. Once he was calm and settled, I sat next to him holding his hand. He drifted in and out of sleep for a few hours, and when he awoke, he said, "You're not a good mother." I was mortified. He was suffering from dementia and we all knew that, but to say that to me when he didn't recognize who I was and thought I was his own daughter (my mother) was more than I could take. Even though I knew he didn't think that way about me, Nola, the hurt of that remark stayed with me for decades.

Aside from planning for my son's birth in August and impending marriage in October, May brought Toni's transplant. Toni and I were close. She was a lovely young girl born in 1970, and she showed me a great deal of respect and love in such a short time of knowing her. Derek, my stepson, was difficult to manage sometimes, mainly due to his mother's adverse comments about the new woman in her soon-to-be-ex-husband's life. He also gave his bone marrow to Toni, which meant his hospitalization was an intensely difficult time for him too. I have to say here that, in observing his biological parents' total focus on Toni, it was not a shock when Derek began to exhibit serious emotional issues when the transplant he had been a donor for didn't work. Neither Derek's mother nor father were giving him any tangible emotional support, nor did they continue to really support him in the right way for many years into his teens, which had major repercussions on him as a young adult. He wet the bed almost constantly, went silent and unresponsive for long periods, and acted up from time to time.

In May, I nearly split from Bill due to the pressure we were all under. We had a long drawn-out silence over Toni's health and his soon-to-be ex-wife's comments. Toni seemed to get so much better after her transplant. She was gaining weight, looking good, gaining energy, and feeling optimistic about the future. By July, she, Derek, and I had really started to connect well. My pregnancy was actually noticeable. My tight abs showed the bump, and I had stopped getting the early onset labor contractions. We had some respite.

But by late July to early August, news of Toni was not good. She had come out of remission again for the fourth and last time. There was nothing more the doctors could do. The transplant had been the last option, and though they thought with a family donor things would've turned out better, Toni and all of us simply had to wait.

Derek withdrew, Bill and I began to provide palliative care to her at our home when she was there, and Toni's mother started to experience all sorts of mood swings, which in turn affected the pending divorce. It made communication between the adults almost impossible to navigate at times. To top it all off, my beloved Pa had died in early August, and his funeral was held about ten days before Nick was born. I could not go and was so upset about that. It was isolating to not be able to be there for my grandma. My own pregnancy history and Toni's fragility meant I had to stay at home. It was one of the saddest times of my life, yet I knew Pa wouldn't hold a grudge. He was always so caring and loving toward me throughout my life despite his serious dementia and Parkinson's disease in later years.

Nick's arrival finally came almost a fortnight earlier than planned. I was in serious labor at home for twelve hours before going to the hospital around 9:00 p.m. on August 19. A home birth had long since been ruled out. Toni and I had been eating pizza and playing backgammon on my bed. Toni was very frail and in a wheelchair most of the time, but we managed to make fun out of what was a distracting and emotional period for all of us. Bill seemed to be quite distant at that time, which was understandable considering how he felt about his daughter—his first-born child and ultimately what I came to realize as the real love of his life.

The labor and birthing experience I actually quite enjoyed, in the end. I played backgammon, a game Jesse's mom had taught me, right up until I was almost fully dilated; a great game to keep your mind off the awkwardness of contractions. I felt in control of what was about to happen for the first time in a long time. I'll never forget the first words that came out of my mouth when Nick was born: "Hello, my beautiful Nicholas Sean." I'd watched Nick being born with a mirror to show me what my body was doing. I was high as a kite on oxygen and just a little Pethidine right at the end. I didn't need an episiotomy, had no stretch marks, and had no after-birth issues. It was an amazing and uplifting experience. After all those months of talking to him and singing to him when he was in utero, I finally had that little bundle in my arms, someone I could enjoy and, hopefully, bring loads of joy to.

Nick was born with some questionable health issues. On his father's side, there had been a string of genetic disorders, stillbirths, major developmental abnormalities, and serious birth defects through all arms of his family. On my side, things were fine. Nick was born with a large birthmark on his left shoulder and the left of his face from cheekbone to jaw. I questioned the birth doctor about the facial mark and was told it would probably sink into his face or, if not, could be removed by plastic surgery. I was mortified thinking that something I'd done, obviously something wrong that I had eaten or drunk, had come out as a mark on my baby boy. Little did I know then how that birthmark would come to change our lives.

Toni was the first in the family to hold Nick after his father and me. Thirty minutes after Nick's birth, Bill went back to our home where Toni was sleeping. Toni needed to be checked on and being left alone in the house was not a good idea. She was in bed when we left, but because she was in a wheelchair during the day, she needed to be taken to the bathroom and bathed first thing in the morning. Bill spent most of the day with Toni, and around 2:00 p.m., he returned with her to the hospital to see Nick and me. Derek wasn't with them. By that stage, Nick had literally disappeared. The nurses had taken him to another ward and another mother. I was mortified and under serious emotional pressure to maintain my composure, not knowing where my new baby had gone. It was four hours before the nurses found Nick. It was an awful time waiting and wondering if he was OK.

Returning home five days later was a welcome relief for me. I loved being a mom, and Nick was thriving. However, the pressure of Toni's ailing health began to take hold of the family again. I have one picture of her nursing Nick at home—we managed to get her into a beanbag by lowering her down from her wheelchair where she was now pretty much spending her whole day. Her limbs were so fragile, her skin so thin that anything beyond featherlike touch could cause severe bruising. Toni and Derek both nursed Nick that day, and the pictures show the happiness and love they felt for him despite the family dynamic and Toni's ailing condition.

Toni weakened as each day passed. Derek became quiet at times and then outspoken and funny at other times. It was a roller coaster like I've never ridden. Nick, a babe in arms, seemed to be riding the tsunami quite well. However, only five weeks after Nick was born, young Toni died at thirteen years of age. In those last few weeks, she spent many hours asleep in her wheelchair. When we finally got her into bed for a night's rest, I would walk past her room regularly to check on her. She would sometimes be awake and call out gently to me, "Hello, Sam, love you." Sam was the nickname she had for me—I never knew where that came from, but I liked it. She rarely ate, but we managed to get some liquids into her and loads of oranges, which she craved. Toni was gradually losing body mass and physical strength, but her mental and emotional strength was there all the way.

Those last few days were a mixture of her dropping in and out of coma-like states, rarely drinking, not eating, and reached the point a day or so before she died where I could hear the death rattle from time to time. Her body odor changed; I knew the end was coming. Her father made the decision to take her back to her mother's place and from there, within a matter of hours, she was placed in the hospital. Bill says he was with her when she died. The blessed, happy little girl had gone from our lives.

Time came for the funeral. I don't recall Bill being involved in organizing it; it seemed to be his first wife's doing. But the hardest part was being told I wasn't to attend. That request gutted me to such a level that I couldn't speak much to anyone when they came back from the funeral. Everyone went except me—friends, family, Bill, Derek, Bill's first wife's friends, and family. But not the woman who had been the loving stepmom for the past and last year of Toni's life. For the life of me, I couldn't work out what monster would ask me to stay away. But I accepted the request as something I just had to endure. Imagine sitting at home alone, with a newborn child, wishing you could be at your stepdaughter's funeral to say farewell and feeling totally disempowered? I don't know how I tolerated that, but I did. I took it as a slap in the face from my soon-to-be husband.

I spent the next couple of weeks finalizing plans for our impending marriage. Anyone else, without a babe in arms, would have long gone. October 22 was the day we married, and it was also my mother's birthday. Mother had been conspicuously absent since paying the deposit on an $800 bridal outfit that she said she would pay for in full, leaving me to pay the balance. She was also nowhere to be seen when it came time to arrange catering, celebrant, and venue. Instead of the wedding I'd always dreamed of, I had to have a wedding on the cheap in our backyard in suburbia with only one of my old friends around, Bill's friends and family, and just a handful of people I knew for more than one year. My brother and Mother came, but attendance by my broader family was not encouraged. Bill also did not allow Derek to attend, a decision that damaged Derek's and Bill's relationship for a long, long time.

My mother looked suspiciously at the wedding cake that she had had no part in organizing, and then half way through the post-wedding reception, she up and left. After what seemed like an hour, I found her standing at her car in the street discussing her birthday gift that she had just been given. She turned to me as I approached and said, "There're other places I could be right now. I've made an effort to come here today. I hope you know that." I was, once again, dumbstruck. Was she seriously blaming me for keeping her from her other commitments? Or was it all about her?

Despite the negative aspects of my wedding day, I did enjoy being married. I had a sense of security in knowing I had rights and responsibilities to fulfill and also a sense of family for the first time since my childhood with Grandma and Pa. There was no honeymoon as a couple and no real wedding night. Remember, I had a two-month-old baby I was still breastfeeding, and he came with us everywhere. Needless to say, when I left my marriage years later, I left the wedding photos behind.

Life after Toni's death and the marriage was a combination of the usual family, young baby, pre-puberty child, financial pressure, and day-to-day things. I found relief and stimulation in both my new child and also some part-time ICT consulting. I planned to stay out of the full-time workforce for five years to give my son the best possible grounding in life. I'd missed out on that time with my own mother, and I didn't want him to have a mom always away at work.

However, the plan for such a long time at home didn't happen as a result of two key things. I was missing adult stimulation, and Bill did not earn enough to sustain us and enable us to grow a better future. Living in suburbia was OK, but not where he wanted to be. We'd already begun while Toni was alive to look for country properties to buy. When the owner of the rental property became too pushy and increased the rent, we used that opportunity to find an affordable two acres in the country in a very small country town. We arranged for a one-door very small transportable cedar cottage to be built and placed on the land. We moved out there, about seventy miles from Canberra, in the February of 1984. Nick was just six months old, and I felt he would also benefit from living in the fresh air and open spaces.

Chapter 16

My career from August 1984 onward certainly started to get back on track after I'd had almost a year's break with Nick at home. My going back to work full-time to my ICT career was not only a way to break free of the small parochial town in which we lived, it was my way of getting back to being with people. I was totally isolated with no close local friends. Every time I'd drive into Canberra with Nick, I wouldn't want to return. The locals in that tiny Aussie town used to call me the "Yank woman." Having lived in Texas, you can imagine how I felt about being called a Yankee.

Living so far out of town and commuting to work every day was exhausting. I was up at 6:00 a.m., dressed, and preparing breakfast ready to leave by seven. I'd drive an hour and a half to the childcare center or daycare, then drive to work, work eight hours, and then reverse repeat of the drive followed by the bedtime routine. But somehow through all of that, Bill and I managed to owner-build a massive mud-brick home by hand, making all the bricks and doing the majority of the construction ourselves. I landscaped the almost two-acre grounds, and people oftentimes asked me to enter the property in garden competitions. We created a large orchard, a small vineyard, a full-sized tennis court, and an above-ground swimming pool with decking and screening all round it. We ran chickens, hens, ducks, one horse named Thomas, a sheep named Annabel who became a favorite with the family, a few different sheep dogs over time, and an in-bred and crazy Jack Russell terrier.

Nick did well in that country environment, and I thrived in the fresh, open air. It was a good contrast to the mental aspects of my new role in ICT and the long daily commute. In early 1984, the town still had the old-style crank phones in each house, and the central community phone exchange had a plug-in/plug-out board. The operator would listen in on phone calls. There was limited privacy. When I'd travel to places like Southeast Asia for business, it was way too much for the operator to cope with, listening in.

By that stage, even after living in the shed and on bigger acres, I found it even harder to adjust to that kind of backward community environment. Compared to Austin, Texas, with cable TV, free local calls, drive-thru banking, and the wonderful life I had in the USA, living in a little Aussie town with a sum total of a few hundred inhabitants scattered over thousands of square miles was like going back to the dark ages. It was several years before the telecommunications were brought up to twentieth-century standards and the crank phones replaced with normal round-dial and handset-style phones.

To bring light relief and find some enjoyment, I got heavily involved with community activities. I spent fourteen years as secretary/treasurer/funds coordinator of the local Progress Association, and worked with Nick's motorcycle racing club doing first aid, track marshaling, and secretarial duties. Organizing community dances and weekend markets kept me busy, as did advocating for community advancement in the face of political and government barriers and in spite of the community constantly changing its mind about what it wanted. I ruffled a few feathers being so American in my manner, hardworking and future-focused. I learned an awful lot about parochial small-town thinking. I also came to appreciate the difficulties faced by legitimately struggling farmers.

I did the bulk of the work in creating and sustaining the first community newspaper; however, the community's demand for gossip over real news and positive information became the point where I bowed out of doing all the marketing, editorial, and typesetting work. My mind-set just didn't match the community. I looked and stepped forward; they stood still and looked back.

From 1984 for three years, I worked in a senior systems engineering and global project management role, traveling extensively and working with senior federal government clients. For quite some time, I managed the company's largest international client from a technical perspective, and I was really having a ball until the management structure of the company changed. The push came for me to become even more technical and go back to the computer programming days that I had long left behind. With a fabulous offer extended to join Price Waterhouse Urwick, the Canberra-based consulting arm of the big international accounting firm, I gladly moved across to them in the latter months of 1987. I have to give special thanks to Derek Boughton for that move. He was a savior at a time when I felt the pressure of gender-based discrimination caving in on me again. Female engineers, then and now, are few and far between.

It was with this move into a senior management and business development role that allowed Bill to retire, as he put it. At thirty-eight, he could be the house-husband, and I would be the sole breadwinner. I earned enough money, but when it came down to it, my work hours had significantly increased. I had little recoup time, and the pressures of too little support from him began to mount again. While he was off playing tennis with the local townswomen during the week days, flirting, swapping recipes, taking Nick to playgroup, and playing around with various hobbies at home, I was working and commuting seventy-five hours a week, doing the household shopping, managing the household finances, and making sure the mortgage was paid. I was having to clean what was not cleaned by him in the house, and provide support to Nick whenever I had a spare minute.

Nick started to suffer migraines in his stomach. When I'd go off to work, Nick would last a few weeks in his father's care then be off to hospital with severe stomach pains. I'd leave my office, travel to the hospital to sort out yet another drama, and shortly after I'd arrive, Nick would settle down and be able to be discharged. It wasn't an attention thing, and the doctors couldn't explain it other than stomach migraines. However, I always felt there was something underlying, and in years to come, I realized it was more my healing manner that Nick responded to rather than the lack of care by his father. I never really knew what was and wasn't happening for Nick at that time. It was very hard not fully trusting your own husband to do the right thing.

Working for Price Waterhouse was a learning and stimulating experience, a different world to ICT even though I was rapidly growing a business area that specialized in recruiting ICT professionals for placement with client organizations. I was also responsible for initiating and growing the human resources consultancy services offered by the firm, and it was due to that aspect that my next major career move into the finance industry occurred. I had managed to get Derek, who'd always shown an interest in my own ICT career, into the Australian government's tax office for a work experience placement. That was the beginning of a sound ICT career for him in both Australia and the UK.

In mid-1988, I had two choices. I was being headhunted by Australia's largest hydroelectric scheme in the Snowy Mountains region to lead their ICT strategy group. The role would see me based closer to the small town that was home. My other choice was to step into a brand-new role in a completely different industry sector than I had ever worked—to spearhead a change program that would bring mammoth changes to the financial institution and its customer base.

By moving from Price Waterhouse to the finance sector, I became one of only two women in Australia to have such a senior role in a male-dominated industry. I had my career sights set on being the CEO of St. George Bank and therefore, heading the HR area, responsible for governance and corporate change as well, seemed a logical step.

That next step to a CEO in the finance sector was not to be, and there were two key reasons. First, workplace bullying, as I later recounted in 2007 to a friend, the current Australian Vice Chief of the Defense Force Air Marshall Mark Binskin. When you're at that level, bullying against women is rife in industry and very cleverly hidden. His knowing comment to me was, "I bet it was." Women in positions of power were seen by many men as a threat. It came to be that the insecure man I worked for in the finance industry did everything in his power, with considerable stealth and premeditation, to undermine every change I heralded. He tried to disrupt my team of capable professionals, discredit me, and make cutting and hurtful comments in every setting.

At one point after a grueling sixteen-hour work day, I inadvertently had my car locked overnight in the parking garage where I routinely kept it. I knocked on his office door, and advised him that I would be in a little later the next day as I was having to stay overnight with friends in the city and would then have to drive an hour and a half home early in the morning to get showered, changed, and then come back to work. He seemed completely disinterested. He made a hugely cutting remark, similar in intent to when he used to come into my office and push all my neatly organized papers off the desk. I was not just shocked, I was deeply hurt. Hurt that such a person was so opposite to everything that I was working hard to create in that financial institution. He was, up until that time, the worst bully I'd ever encountered in the workplace.

Combined with this toxic workplace treatment and many times feeling like I was climbing Mount Everest instead of changing an organizational culture, at this same time a whole bunch of stuff was happening in my life. My parents-in-law both passed away suddenly only six weeks apart in time. They were in my father's age group and almost as frail as my grandmother. My mother was almost destitute and did not speak up about it to anyone. She'd had a long battle to get a workplace compensation claim agreed to by the public service, and I had to step in and advocate for her with the government compensation regulatory body to enable her to receive ongoing payments and large back payments. My own sentiment is that she was imagining a lot of the allergy symptoms and creating the illness to suit her needs, but challenging her motives was like opening a hornet's nest. She was determined to "make the government pay" for her perceived illnesses.

My mother, having not been to a doctor for a pap smear in some thirty years, had developed highly invasive B2-grade cervical cancer. She refused chemotherapy and was headed for the operating theatre on short notice for a radical hysterectomy. I was the only person available to assist her in managing everything associated with that.

Nick's facial birthmark was starting to change, which was not a good sign, and my beloved grandma was hospitalized with a return of bowel cancer. She died a few weeks later.

Coupled with Nick's frequent trips to the hospital, my husband's lack of understanding with respect to the demands on my being in such a senior role, and his lack of tangible support on the home front, the three deaths in a short timeframe, coupled with the illness and domestic situation of my mother, it was all I could do to keep all the balls in the air and not lose the plot myself. I knew I was strong, but that time tested me like no other before it.

One night amidst all of that, I made the fatal mistake of taking a phone call one evening from a trusted female colleague who unbeknown to me had been undermining me behind my back. I broke down in tears on the phone. The grief, loss, and other loads were collectively overwhelming. She listened, of course, taking it all in. I had to be absent to take care of my grandma and my mother. I was constantly in dialogue with obstructive public servants about the compensation payments, attending funerals, cleaning my mother's home, and having everything set up for her return after surgery. Every waking hour outside of my senior executive role was spent either busy or away with family, especially on weekends. Instead of the company offering for me to have some compassionate leave, within a month I was feeling the pressure to leave that role.

The so-called friend on the phone had been positioning herself to create a more junior HR management role, and ultimately, that is what occurred. Many of the staff, the people who knew what I was looking to achieve and had seen the positive changes I'd embedded, were collectively gutted when I left. After leaving that high-profile role, I had a few weeks with my husband to attend to outstanding property matters and possessions held at his late parents' home in outback New South Wales. I spent a few days just chilling out in my head. Where was my career going now? Being at the top isn't any good when the support system isn't strong enough to help you get through all the challenges that come with such senior roles. Once again, I felt like it just wasn't worth the effort on my part. Sure, I had earned good money, but I was aged in a way that I didn't like. I looked a lot older and weathered than my young thirty-three years. I was more middle-aged than young—where had my youth gone?

Chapter 17

In 1989, prior to leaving the finance industry, I used some personal funds to finance a trip back to Texas. Up until that time, no one there was stopping me from having contact with Jesse or his family. I contacted people in advance of that trip to plan visits to key people. I had only six days in Texas and arrived in Austin. A girlfriend there had, by that stage, divorced her husband and was living in an apartment with her seven-year old son. I stayed there one night and then met up with another friend near New Braunfels. We had a lovely visit for a couple of days, and then I was driven to Sealy to see Jesse's daddy, stepmom, and sister. It was there that Jesse met up with me. The plan was for me to travel to Houston to spend a little time with him, and then onto Flatonia the next day to visit with another girlfriend.

For all those years of loving Jesse, my seeing him was even harder than leaving before. I wanted to get closure on my feelings for him, so that I could at least have my heart back. But that trip in 1989 just reinforced to me how much I loved him at a deep soul level that even I can't explain.

I had photographs to show to everyone there. I met his sister's first-born little boy, and I could also see that visit was difficult for Jesse. I was very much into children and babies at that stage. I focused on his sister's little boy and being friendly to everyone in the room instead of just on Jesse, and while it was not deliberate on my part, I think that might have hurt him. Despite that hiccup, Jesse took me onto Houston, and we met up with a number of his friends and had a fun night out. He took me back to my hotel, and if there was ever a moment I wanted to tell him how I felt, how much I loved him, and how I didn't want to go back to Australia, it was then. But I was silent, and went back to my room alone and remained deeply torn about what to do. Jesse didn't make any motion toward me, but from what I could see, we enjoyed that time together. It was a real joy for me to be with him.

The visit in Flatonia went really well. We went to Nuevo Laredo, Mexico, for the day with two of my girlfriend's teacher friends. I must have flown out of Houston; I don't remember all the details. I do remember having a sense of déjà vu on the plane going back to Australia though.

The relief on Bill's face when I arrived was obvious. He was waiting at the airport for me with Nick, and life just kept going on as usual. I didn't get closure with Jesse emotionally, and yet I was happy to be back with my beautiful son. It was all topsy-turvy again. My heart still reached out to Jesse.

By late March of 1990, within a very short time of finishing in the finance industry role, I had pretty much walked into a senior role in state government community health. The role had huge responsibilities. I could apply my advanced management techniques to make great changes and improvements, but it was based locally and close to home. I felt like I was being pushed down that dead-end path again. Even though my senior colleagues in the health sector all predicted my becoming CEO of the local large hospital, I couldn't see that as anything other than a dead-end career move.

My time in the state government health system was fruitful, educational, and full of variety. It was a challenging role and a whole lot of fun despite my reservations and career concerns. I managed many clinical health practitioners—mental health nurses, specialists, educators, speech pathologists, and audiometrists. I liaised with key government and medical personnel, such as police, doctors, specialists, educators, and crisis center workers. We did some wonderful work in the community, and I made some very positive changes in the system. My colleagues and department were impressed and pleased.

But for all the positives, the one negative and lingering aspect was having to be involved in the scheduling of a distressed young mother to a mental institution. Brought on by her bad behavior, the police and mental health team perceived mistreatment of her young child. That day I realized I'd been a party to completely changing the outcome of someone's life—her being scheduled for psychiatric assessment and treatment at one of the state's largest institutions. It took me a long time to come to terms with how my positional power had impacted another human being.

Knowing that my position required me to make sometimes difficult, life-changing decisions was one of the factors in deciding to step out on my own to start my own consulting business again. I really didn't feel comfortable being involved in such a stressful cycle of decision-making. To potentially change someone's life in such a negative way, even as a result of their own bad actions, was not a role that I wanted. In 1990, after only eight short months at Health, I began my part-time consulting practice. Within a week, I was back in the same department providing strategic planning, facilitation, ICT, and policy support to my colleagues at the state level.

My next eight years of consulting work began. It was an empowering and fulfilling period, yet at times frustrating given that I was physically located so far from any major cities. I had many clients in government and industry, and I did some great advocacy work in the environmental protection space. I introduced new systems, policies, strategies, training programs, and business plans to many entities that truly needed the help.

In the late 1980s and early 1990s, life was pretty challenging for the family in managing Derek's needs. He approached me in 1987, asking if it was OK if he lived with us in the country. I said of course, but I also opened his eyes to the reality of life commuting into Canberra every day: long days, lots of driving, and isolation. He was not getting along with his mother at that time and was obviously missing us. Ultimately Derek decided to stay with his mother. We had many deep and meaningful moments and discussions, but the topic that stood out the most was his view on being biologically connected.

When Derek was about sixteen years old, he commented to me that being biologically connected doesn't mean you have to care about the person. At the time, I thought, *How awful and callous*, but over time I've come to realize he was right. My grandma always pushed us to keep the family together and talking, but when people consistently don't see eye to eye, are fundamentally different in their values, and cover up or hide hurtful events just to keep face with others, there's absolutely no point putting yourself through that trauma of staying connected just for family's sake.

After I'd sent a Christmas card in 1989 saying how much I'd enjoyed the visit to Texas, Jesse's stepmom wrote back to me. She explained that my visit had caused Jesse great distress, and that he was going to be marrying one of his cousins from Louisiana in the near future. She said it would be best if I no longer contacted any of them. As a result of that letter from her, I ceased all communication and did my best to put the past and my love for him well and truly to rest. To help myself through that confusing and traumatic time, I allowed my heart to freely love him, but in my head I imagined he was in another world, and there was no chance of ever seeing him again. That was the only way I could see to live the rest of my life with any level of happiness and sense of peace.

I became heavily involved in Nick's grade school—volunteering for canteen duty, library help, and also tutoring students in math, reading, and spelling. I spent a lot more time with Nick once I'd left full-time work, and Bill was eventually happy to go back to work himself. During that time, I had wanted to have another child. Bill had arranged a vasectomy six months after Toni died against the advice of his own doctor and certainly against my wishes. By the time I'd stopped working and was enjoying spending time at home with Nick, I began to long for another baby. Bill was well over forty by that stage and dead set against any more kids though he did consider a reversal of the vasectomy at one point. He claimed bad genes as his reason for his desire of having no more children. Our communication about key issues had sunk to a low point once again.

Nick was the one I'd talk to about things when he slept. Nick saw me cry a few times, and he would always give me a hug and say, "Mummy, please don't cry. It'll be alright." At that time, Derek and I were also very close. On one of his visits, he accidentally stepped in on me crying in private. He knew that something wasn't right, and I confided in him that I wasn't happy with his father, I wanted more children, and I would never be able to have them.

Derek was genuinely caring and shared a lot of what he knew about his father. That was a reassuring time, knowing my son and stepson were there for me. I also confided some of my concerns with a male friend in the village in which we lived. People ultimately misconstrued the connection we had and read way more into that friendship than should have been read. I've never been impressed when people make assumptions—assumptions openly voiced can damage other people in various ways.

On the positive side, as a family, we really did do a lot of happy things together—camping, caravanning, and visiting other states of Australia. We had many dinner parties, and as I've often said and made clear to others, it wasn't all bad. There were some very funny moments, and some pleasurable events that took place over the course of my marriage. When I left the marriage, it was a total and utter shock to many, many people. We had appeared, in public, an everyday married couple. I kept a whole lot to myself, like my feelings for Jesse, and while Bill and I lived with largely different values, we did agree to disagree on many things that made life livable. He knew that if he treated Nick the way his mother had treated him, with physical abuse, then I would leave with Nick without hesitation. Many times I had to stand between Nick and Bill.

I suffered a number of personal health challenges over those first ten years with Bill—early menopause symptoms, cellular activity that signaled a cancer was about to take hold in my body, heavy menstrual cycles, severe headaches and migraines, night sweats coupled with bad nightmares, and flashbacks of events through my life. My undiagnosed PTSD symptoms were getting worse, and I didn't realize it.

In what I thought was the last ditch effort to connect with Bill, I arranged a reaffirmation of vows in 1993. Little did I know that Bill had been seeing an old friend from work for many years, confiding in her and asking her advice. The reaffirmation of vows, while a real effort for me given that I loved Jesse, was not a good surprise for Bill either. It was not something he'd initiated, and therefore he was not in control.

We stumbled through that event, appropriately supported by friends and family, with Bill's next wife being the one to read aloud a poem Bill had written years earlier during the ceremony. I really was living a sham of a marriage, but I was determined to do all that I could to make the happy times more frequent and to turn things around. I believed in the institution of marriage and wanted to honor the effort and work that is expected as far as I humanly could.

Chapter 18

A few short years after leaving government health and starting my part-time consulting work again, I was also beginning the journey of working in client-based health and rehabilitation by gaining qualifications in the traditional therapies, a long-held dream of mine. In 1974, I had my heart set on going to Melbourne University and studying to become a physiotherapist when I'd finished high school. I felt that gaining qualifications in traditional medicine across a broad spectrum of areas would allow me to help people holistically. I commenced studying in late 1995, opened a clinic in the local town where I worked, and within eighteen months, I had my qualifications, accreditation to the Australian Traditional Medicine Society, and a strong clientele. At last, I had the time and energy to help others in a way that was immensely fulfilling to me.

By early 1996, with Nick getting older and the marriage not going anywhere positive, I had a contingency plan worked out to achieve a break from Bill. For many years after we moved to that little town, I'd been phone-calling Jesse's half-brother and staying in touch with other family members. It seemed right in my heart to do that, to stay connected with them. But I knew it was contributing to the wedge that had always been between Bill and me.

By 1996, I was really only focused on making sure I could provide for Nick and me without undue hardship. The plan was in place; I was set to leave. Then Bill had a heart attack in early June 1996. For two years prior, Bill had been having chest pain and not said anything to me about it. He kept saying the pain was stomach related. He drank copious quantities of coffee each day, smoked many cigarettes, and was very stressed at work. His consumption of alcohol was also a concern. His alcohol-based relief from emotional pain had been obvious from when I first met him in 1982, and in 1984, he drank himself into a stupor before admitting Toni's death meant the end of his world as he knew it. From 1984 on, he seemed to be in self-destruct mode. I always knew Nick, Derek, and I took a sad second place to her memory. She meant more to him than anyone ever could or would.

Nick stayed with some friends that day in June while I drove Bill to rendezvous forty miles away with the ambulance coming from Canberra. Bill was very distressed, and I was in logistics and patient management mode. His heart attack was managed, and he spent about a week in hospital having various tests before he was found to be in need of intervention surgery. After that first traumatic week in Canberra, not knowing if he was going to live or die, the hospital being so negative and critical about his health and the root causes of his atherosclerosis, and Nick and I having to stay with friends in Canberra while we waited for news, we returned back to the mud-brick home in the country.

So began a couple of months of intensive home care by me to keep Bill alive and get him strong enough for surgery in Sydney. When the time came for surgery, Nick was already taking time off from high school. He had been significantly disrupted emotionally and mentally by what had happened to his father. The heart attack had caused all sorts of transport issues, and Nick was not coping with having to get the bus home part of the way or be dropped at school by someone else instead of me, a trip that lasted over two hours. It was extremely difficult to juggle the need to care for Bill at home and make sure Nick's life wasn't turned upside down.

Our diet drastically changed. Bill refused to eat any flesh of any kind—no fish, no chicken, no beef. We began counting fat grams, eliminating all salt and sugar, and introduced tofu. I finally put my foot down and started cooking completely different meals for Bill. He wouldn't speak about how he felt. He just focused on himself and sort of withdrew into a shell. He was weak, unconfident, stressed, and easily upset at even the slightest thing. It was like a completely different person was emerging.

Driving down for his surgery a couple of months later to Sydney, we stayed with friends close to the hospital. However, Bill's surgery didn't go as planned. He went in for an angioplasty but suffered a cardiac arrest in the post-op recovery room. He was defibrillated back to life, had been in cell acidosis mode, and was dead for well over three minutes. He was returned to the operating room and had very long stents placed in the worst of his arteries—an experimental surgery being done by St. Vincent's Hospital.

I'd been away having lunch at a café in Kings Cross, a sleazy inner-city suburb neighboring the hospital. At exactly the time of the cardiac arrest, I looked up at a clock on the wall at the moment Bill arrested. I remember thinking that something was not right. I'd not had a phone call confirming he was out of surgery. I walked quickly back to the hospital and started asking questions, and I received a number of fob-offs and nonanswers from medical staff.

Finally the doctors admitted to me what had happened. They had performed an angioplasty, and the surgery had been too much of a shock for his heart. He had gone into fibrillation, and they were lucky to get him back. It was a long wait in intensive care before I got to see Bill in the middle of the night. He was lying in bed and looked grey as a corpse, felt cold as ice, and smelled like the corpse I had seen in Canberra all those years earlier. I was shocked and unsure what to think. I read enough of his chart and the treatments he'd received to arm myself with information for later research.

The hospital did not expect him to survive. The arrest had been severe, and his artery was fragile. I managed to get in touch with Derek via Derek's new stepfather, and explained that he should come and see his dad as soon as possible. Derek hadn't been very close to his father for many years, but I'm glad he came that day. He had a lather of perspiration when he entered his father's room in ICU. Nick was there too and the boys and I all went downstairs to have a cup of tea and something to eat in the cafeteria of the hospital.

After the visit, Derek returned to Canberra and Nick was collected by my friends for the night. They both seemed to be coping OK, although for Derek it was seeing his father's fragility that was the greatest shock.

After a couple of days, Bill was moved to a normal ward, and it was then that I realized he was really different. He made no sign of love or affection toward me, and showed no interest in my being there at all. At one point, he couldn't remember my name when some friends came to visit him. I was sitting in the chair, and he didn't know my name. Gone was the man I had known, and along had come the new spirit, a soul reborn—a callous, cold, and distant man with dead eyes. His eyes were the mirror to his soul, and they were milky and clouded like a shark's eyes—dead.

So the new journey together began.

Chapter 19

The day we left the Sydney hospital, I drove Bill, Nick, and I across the harbor bridge to our friend's house. Bill described me as the "three-minute widow." I didn't understand what he meant. He laughed and said, "Like boiling an egg for three minutes, you were a widow for three minutes." It took years for me to realize that the 'til-death-do-us-part aspect of my marriage vows had come and gone. I was still legally married to a man I really didn't love anymore, and he was now a total stranger.

He kept talking about seeing Toni while he was in cardiac arrest, but what he described didn't make sense. His story kept changing, depending on who he spoke to. He seemed really cocky and had such a super ego; it was almost nauseating to see him in action with other men being so competitive and with women so flirtatious. I wondered what my real role was meant to be now.

We returned to our mud-brick home in the dead of winter. People stayed away. I don't think friends really knew what to do to help. Bill was very unwell, and for the next two years I didn't actually have a full night's sleep. For the first few months when he was still recuperating and getting strong enough to return to work, if I ever had to be absent away from home for short periods, I would arrange for someone to come to the house to sit with him until I got back. If I had to take Nick to school, I would always arrange to have someone on standby for Bill.

Bill now suffered from sleep apnea, and I literally lay awake listening to him breathing for two years. I would micro-sleep sitting upright a lot of the time. If his breathing became too shallow or stopped, I would shake him to wake him up and start him breathing again. I used acupressure, lymphatic drainage, and other gentle massage to help him at physical and mental levels. The hospital rang in the second month to check if he was still alive. They clearly had not expected him to live; the stent procedure was unproven. He had essentially been one of their successful guinea pigs.

Bill returned to work after about three months' recuperation, and he was on fairly heavy medication to keep his cardiovascular system in good condition. Six months after his surgery and cardiac arrest, I sat down with him and explained how I felt. He seemed to really not understand and was even more in a selfish space. All he could think about was changing our lives and his work to suit his illness, his new dynamic, his recovery, and his future. There was never once an open acknowledgment that Nick and I were there along with him. Our needs were irrelevant. His work colleagues saw a different side of him too. They stayed away where previously they had been happy to come and visit. If Bill was talking, it certainly wasn't to me.

If you could imagine a child's development—from birth through the years—that is what it was like with Bill at home. From his cardiac arrest, he behaved for the most part like a child growing up. When the terrible twos came, he was just like a temperamental toddler with screaming fits and tantrums. In the second year after surgery, he suddenly decided that he needed to manage his own medications. At that point, I knew that one day in the foreseeable future, I would not be needed at all—it would be time for me to leave. I also knew I'd have to leave for my own sanity and emotional health.

In January 1998, with the inconvenience of having to live so far away from Canberra, Nick's school, and Bill's cardiologist, our home finally sold after some two years of advertising and waiting. I wanted to move to civilization again. Nick had new friends in Canberra and was feeling isolated in the country. Bill was not happy with the idea, but he agreed that moving closer to schools and hospital was a better outcome for everyone. That was the first sign ever that I'd seen him consider our needs too.

We moved to a smaller home not far from the Canberra hospital. It had a large in-ground pool in the backyard, which Bill could exercise in, and things seemed to go along quite well. I re-established my clinic, but by July, Bill was having stress issues again. I decided that his health situation was too precarious for me to continue self-employment. In August 1998,

I joined the government workforce. At that time, I was also a board member at Nick's high school, my old high school, and treasurer of the canteen. I was busy doing volunteer work again that I loved.

I enjoyed being back in the normal workforce, and after six months in the role, I felt even more stabilized about the future. For the first time, I felt I had real financial control of Nick's and my future in the event of Bill's death. My work was in the health and safety strategic advisory space. I loved it. Again I began to get involved in professional bodies, offering volunteer services, and continued my clinic until finally handing over clients to other therapists about a year later. The consulting stopped about that time too. At one stage, the college where I'd studied natural therapies had me return to supervise their student practice clinic on a Saturday. I thoroughly enjoyed the adult educator aspects of that work and was feeling so good that they had chosen me. I'd been one of their better students and achieved high marks; I was pretty confident that I'd found my niche in life once again.

But with my return to work and the long hours involved, the distance seemed to get bigger and bigger between Bill and me. Nick was having some issues at high school, and Bill seemed to grow more dissatisfied with life. I know I was dissatisfied as a wife and had been for many years. Something had to give. I came up with the idea that we should sell up in suburbia and move back to the country—find some acreage where Nick could ride motorcycles again more easily, Bill could be in his element, and I could grow fresh vegetables and have a large garden again. I was getting desperate for a solution by that stage. I thought that a new home would mean our marriage issues might be fixable. How wrong I was.

In 1999, we sold the Canberra home having made some substantial improvements and improving our capital reserves a little. We moved into a rental home in a suburb closer to where Nick was in senior high school (college) and finally found forty-two acres at Michelago, not far from Canberra. We engaged a builder and project-managed the build between us.

While still renting in Canberra, I felt compelled to visit with a plastic surgeon to discuss the birthmark on Nick's face. In 1985, I'd been on a plane going to Perth and met a plastic surgeon. He insisted that surgery done early would leave a little, if any, scar. I was hesitant at that time when Nick was a toddler.

The mark had started changing shape when Nick was seven or eight years old. I was concerned that something wasn't right, and that the birthmark might interfere with Nick's love life. It was a very noticeable and large birthmark. The plastic surgeon we ultimately went with said he could certainly remove it, and he suggested we also have the one on his arm removed and biopsied as well. Nick was handling the whole situation really well and went through the surgery with no complications. I had one of the longest cries of my life when he was coming out of the anesthesia, and he touched his face where the mark had been. Instead of the birthmark, there was now a long incision all the way down his face. As his face would grow, so would that new mark. What was done was done. I'd felt bad for years thinking that I'd done something to create the birthmark in the first place, but everyone I spoke to said that birthmarks happen for a range of reasons and it was not my fault.

It was a week or so later, after the biopsy results had come in and our return visit to the specialist that Nick and I got our biggest wake-up call. The facial birthmark had been malignant and was going to kill him sooner rather than later. I was shocked; Nick was calm and quiet. We went on to discuss the likely prognosis—a good one considering the depth of tissue that the surgeon had taken. Each year that passed after that I was more and more relieved.

Living in the country again seemed to give Bill a new lease on life. It was more physically demanding on him, but he was pretty strong in his determination to stay well this time around. Nick was delighted in having somewhere large and open to ride his motorcycle on man-made tracks. The views from that property were truly majestic—the mountains that were tipped with snow in winter, all the trees and wildlife, and from Nick's bedroom window, the most beautiful view of the countryside.

In the year 2000, from September to December, the country seemed to be a cure all for us even though we were lacking some fundamental things to make life easier—a clothesline, curtains, a ramp into the garage so that we could park our cars, and a decent all-weather access road from the gate.

Then the rain came. It flooded the property when the dam overflowed, the dirt road to the house got cut off, cars got bogged on the road, frustration mounted, and tempers flared. Nick was struggling to stay committed to college, and I was feeling trapped again. I was trapped in a family dynamic that wasn't working for me as much as I'd worked at making it a better one. I was feeling so frustrated and without a purpose in the marriage.

The month of January of 2001 came, and I had begun my move to the spare room of the home. I was off on a business trip that next week. The trip was such a fun time. I didn't miss Bill one bit. I was with guys from work who made me laugh, were interested in me as a person, and were really intelligent, and I was doing exciting and active outdoor activities. We flew sorties in a small search and rescue (SAR) plane 100 feet off the water assessing risk, and I watched the dropping of SAR equipment into the ocean. We were able to be physical every day, boating way out to sea to open sea fish. We travelled out to sea to pick up the SAR gear that had been dropped in the ocean by our work colleagues in the plane. We laughed each night over dinner and each morning over breakfast.

On the second night there, I had a visit to my room by a friend and colleague with whom I had a few interesting conversations. It was clear that we were attracted to one another. What ensued was what I needed, and what he wanted too. For the first time in over a decade, I had real sex and felt truly appreciated. I felt attractive again. It had been so long since I felt attractive to a man, I'd pretty much forgotten how good it felt to feel attractive. Jesse was long in my past, and Bill had never been a lover. I felt like a real woman again.

My return to the country property after that trip meant one thing and one thing only—I was going to leave soon. It was just a matter of time. I started to gather my thoughts, personal items, and began to work through my emotions. I started to look for places to rent and discussed a temporary stay with a distant relative who lived in close-by NSW.

The day I left my marriage in March 2001 was the anniversary of Toni's birthday. I had gotten to the point, chain-smoking seventy-five cigarettes a day for two months, where I just had to get out and away. I had been living in the spare room since January, taken off my wedding ring, and couldn't stand Bill being in my presence. I was torn between staying for Nick and being his mom under very strained and dysfunctional circumstances and leaving.

The preceding weekend had been filled with going through possessions one by one, deciding which of us would keep what, but never once was I allowed in the garage. The garage was where the fishing rod my beloved Pa had given me was kept with all the tackle. They stayed with Bill.

Friends showed up that weekend. I was constantly crying; the thought of leaving my son Nick was really hard. My eyes puffed like a blowfish, and when they asked Bill, "Can't you stop this?" he seemed to be in a mental vacuum somewhere else. Bill and I had earlier discussed separating at the end of the year if things didn't get better between us, but when I decided to leave earlier than that, he went into one of his usual rages. He was no longer in control of me. He could sense that I had fully taken back control of my own life. He didn't like the feeling that he couldn't call the shots anymore.

Over that weekend prior to leaving, considering Nick was going to be staying with his father, I wrote a formal letter giving Bill custodial rights over Nick. That was the worst decision I could have made. Within a few months, Bill removed Nick from his senior college and forced Nick to get a job and help pay the bills—just like Bill's parents had done to him. He repeated the same mistake, but the consequences were tenfold worse.

After the removal truck had left, I drove away from that acreage in the mountains and away from the magnificent views that would have been worth millions in years to come. I felt like a bird released from her cage. I felt free to create a new life for the first time in decades. The eighteen years feeling caged with my wings clipped had made me into a martyr. I hadn't seen it really clearly until then. It was like a festering sore that finally got so infected it had to be removed by major excision. It felt good once the infected life was behind me.

I went straight to the storage unit to have my personal items and a few pieces of furniture offloaded by the removal truck. I'd left most of the furniture in the home with Bill and Nick, taking only a few items. I had to purchase the other furniture I needed myself. I pretty much started afresh.

I cared deeply about Bill when times were tough, when he lost his daughter, when he first had surgery, and through the losses and trials of our marriage. I was always the stronger of the two, and I felt too much like I had to be in the motivational lead with everything. His deficiencies and indiscretions were too many and too deep for me to tolerate, and he always managed to swiftly negate the nice things he said by being cutting and mean when things were not going the way he wanted.

I was never in love with Bill; he was never what I would call a real love. I didn't love him that way, and in fact, I didn't love him at all for most of the latter years of our marriage. I was in the marriage out of a sense of duty to him and my son, fulfilling the vows I had made during our wedding. All the while I loved Jesse. To that extent, perhaps I had been unfaithful all along—unfaithful in my thoughts.

I have said many times I would never repeat the mistake of marrying someone when I love another. However, I can appreciate that for some, loving two people at once can work if the circumstances are more controlled and clear. The lessons I brought forward relate more to the importance of taking time to choose a life partner. That life partner person needs to be as much as possible the right person—one who makes you feel good, will allow you to be yourself yet still change and evolve over time, will be loyal and faithful, the one you would be prepared to die for if need be, someone who gives and receives in equal balance without keeping a tally, not egotistical, not competitive in your relationship.

The little signs that a relationship is based on different fundamental values is a warning that it is likely to be an unfaithful relationship. My ex-husband's blatant disrespect of me in public, his humiliation and embarrassment of me in public, his antagonistic and provocative manner, his lack of self-control, and his blatant control and mental and emotional abuse of me were all things I came to loathe about him.

Nearly two years after I left late in 2002, after my healing sessions and new life beginning, I met with him over coffee to attempt to become friends for Nick's sake. I explained that two months before I left the family home, after I had separated and moved into the spare bedroom, I'd slept with a work colleague during a work trip interstate. He said he completely understood. He and I had not had any sexual relations or intimacy of any kind for many, many years. His sexual preferences from the late 1980s were getting more and more what I would call homosexual in nature. On many occasions up until about 1994, sex between us was nonconsensual, due to me being under duress, and completely lacking any intimacy that one would normally see between husband and wife.

That day over coffee, he admitted to me like a confession, "You know I always criticized you because you have to criticize something that's perfect!" I was dumbstruck, once again. What a weak excuse for being someone's constant critic. My opinion of him fell again, and the more I looked, the more I could see how being with him had been a mammoth mistake that I'd been reluctant to really fix. I had seen all the signs back in 1982, and I chose to either ignore or tolerate them.

My last picnic with Pa in Sydney, November 1982.
He died the following August.

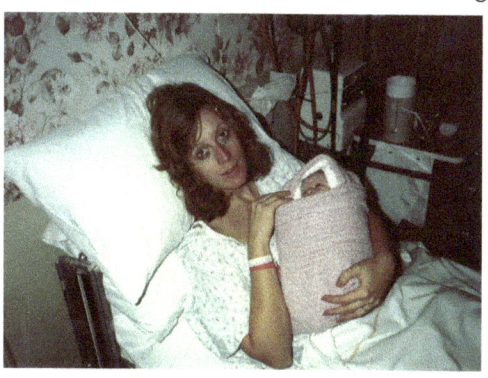

My son, Nicholas Sean, in my arms, August 20, 1983

Late stepdaughter, Toni, nursing baby brother Nick, August 1983

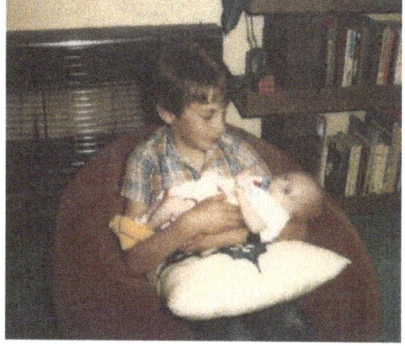

Late stepson, Derek, nursing baby brother Nick, August 1983

With Grandma and Nick, October 1983

Nick's first time travelling into outback NSW, Christmas 1983

Playing with five-month-old Nick, January 1984

With Nick at our country property, December 1984

Not far from our country home, on the shores of the Murrumbidgee River NSW, April 1984

Nick's first time on a merry-go-round, Christmas Eve 1984

On Bicheno Beach TAS, February 1986

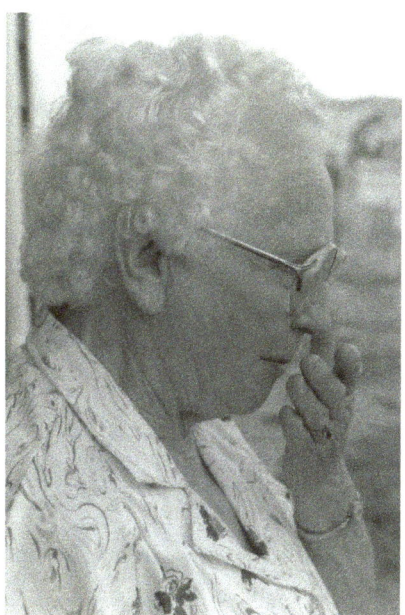

My beautiful, gracious grandma c. 1985

On one of our country picnics in the Snowy Mountains region, winter 1986

Nola Anne Hennessy

Fun with Nick in Wellington Park NSW, October 1987

Nick's first motorbike he raced— a Yamaha PW50, 1989

At Melbourne Zoo, October 1992

On a business trip to Singapore, October 1986

In my PWC office, February 1988

With the carriage driver in Nuevo Laredo, Mexico, July 1989

On holiday at Noosa Heads QLD, February 1994

On a hiking trip at Thredbo NSW, February 1993

With Nick at Dubbo Zoo NSW, April 1995

Visiting Haberfield
Demonstration School,
April 1995

Derek, 23, and Nick, 13, just after
their father's heart surgery,
August 1996

Before my 1st SAREX sortie, goofing around with a colleague, January 2001

Inside the SAR plane during that sortie, facing backwards, which is a fast and guaranteed way to become nauseous. I couldn't eat for hours.

Having fun with Nick's school friend Amy at a motorbike race meeting, c. 1997–98

At my first Defence Officers' Mess Ball, New Parliament House, Canberra 2004

With Nick at the Australian launch of my first two books, December 2009

With my fellow finalists, including Gabi Hollows, at the Rotary International Inspirational Women of 2011 Awards Night in Sydney, March 2011

Dad, Robert Alexander Hennessy, in his late sixties

Chapter 20

The subsequent property settlement was 50 percent to each, but for a long time, Bill lied to people saying, "She cleaned me out." He even said it in front of me at a funeral, a trip that I had personally funded his attendance to, paid for his plane flight, and rented us a car. He was always the one making out that life was worse for him, pushing for the sympathy response, and telling the world he was a victim of circumstance. He was emotionally manipulative and as cunning as a sewer rat by that stage.

My actual divorce was pretty seamless with no animosity. We both got lawyers, and they really didn't do much other than discuss splitting the property. I filed for divorce soon after I left the family home in 2001.

Most of 2001, being away from Bill was a relief. However, I rarely saw Nick. For whatever his father had said or because of how he felt, Nick wouldn't come near me very often. I made the effort I could, avoiding contact with Bill at every opportunity. From the month of March onward, I'd arranged for a part of my salary to be directly paid to Nick's bank so that he was taken care of while still a minor. It was the call from his college after he'd been removed by Bill that stunned me the most, and I realized I had to make things better. I pulled out all stops to stay connected and spent time with him at every chance. That was hard to achieve. He had a mobile phone, but he was difficult to catch. Those first few months were very tough for both of us, and we were apart for a lot of that time.

Having to spend Christmas in 2001 with a cousin in Sydney without Nick was upsetting to me. I felt I was losing my son through his father's manipulation, lies, and the physical distance between us. I rang a family contact to find a good counselor in Sydney who was far away from Canberra. I wanted some privacy to talk through and gain closure on stuff from the past. The family member insisted that a hypnotherapist friend was brilliant and could help.

In February 2002, I decided to undergo hypnotherapy sessions in Sydney. I wanted to be released from forty-five years of emotional baggage and tiredness that I'd accumulated. It was a heavy weight on me that I wanted to be free of once and for all. I had already stepped forward to a better life by leaving my soul-destroying marriage and an unhappy, domestic life. I wanted to be baggage free to explore life and find happiness in ways I'd never known before. I wanted to grow and change to become someone who could do something really good for others. I applied for leave from work and set off to Sydney.

Little did I know how my life would transform in 2002, almost overnight. With a so-called brilliant hypnosis practitioner,

I underwent many sessions of memory regression—going over old memories and reliving the emotions attached to those memories. I started at the present and worked backward in time as I grew stronger and more able to cope with what I was reliving. It was not very pleasant at times; I can surely vouch for that. I learned ways to let go of deep-seated pain, forgive others for making some really dumb decisions that impacted me in ways they never imagined, and forgive all the most significant people in my life who had been either directly responsible for hurting me or responsible by virtue of being inept or silent.

Those intensive long sessions occurred over only a few short weeks during March 2002. I stayed at my mother's place for the first couple of nights. She took me to the first session and was clearly very afraid of what was to take place. My normal medical doctor in Canberra had cautioned me that memory recall usually occurs under hypnosis, and I assured my general practitioner I needed to undertake something that would relieve me of the sadness of my life and the baggage I knew I was needlessly carrying.

I really enjoyed the first session, and I came out feeling light and free in many of my thoughts. In that session, I mastered the letting-go aspect that prevents so many people from dropping into a deep hypnotic trance. I was open to new experiences, and I was open to allowing myself to heal at a deep soul level. My mother, as pushy as she was, just wouldn't back off. She pestered me for information and got in my personal space so much so that after that session, with my karmic intuition starting to work really strongly, I could actually feel her negative energy. I could feel her fear, her control, her power issues, and her anger coming out of her body and straight at me. What was she frightened I'd find out? Even then I must have known deep down that she knew there was a bloody big secret getting ready to be exposed.

In the next hypnosis session, I journeyed to a place of deep inner peace where I could heal myself from the mountain of painful memories I had carried around as emotional baggage for decades. While in the beautiful serenity of space and time that hypnosis brings, all the people who had ever hurt me or done wrong by me were "brought to the campfire"—my choice of a suitable meeting place. This was an action that I facilitated myself; the hypnotherapist merely got me to the right place of subconscious focus. I could do the rest.

At the campfire, I explained to each of them what they had done wrong, how I felt, and that I was going to forgive them and let go of the pain associated with them. They left the campfire slowly without uttering a sound—each of them, one by one. I also used the visualization of tearing pages from my "book of life" as a way of releasing the load borne of those painful memories. As I went through each painful memory, I tore a sheet of paper from the book, mentally placed the pain of the memory on the sheet, and then let the sheet go. I watched them float up to the sky, lightly dancing on each breeze that passed. With each sheet I tore out, my pain reduced and my baggage load got lighter. I went through many memories reclined in that chair in her office, and I continued the same technique at night in the comfort of my bed where I could be alone, quiet, and undisturbed by outside influences.

The letting-go process went on for a number of days. I was exhausted at the volume of memories, but I grew more motivated to continue as the lightness and freedom that I felt was the greatest feeling. I learned, through choosing my own colors and methods, how to draw greater volumes of energy into my body from the universe around me. This technique I had previously used when delivering Reiki—channeling good universal energy—for my clients, so I knew exactly what I needed to do for myself. I simply opened my mind to allowing good energy to come to me personally, where previously I had drawn it in for others.

As a consequence of allowing in the good energy, it felt like the full width of my head was the funnel through which the energy came. I could see it in my mind and feel it happening in my head and through my body. I could do nothing to stop it once it had started. Good universal energy filled every cell and structure in my body. I felt amazing and full of love for everything and everyone.

Once I'd drawn in all the good energy my body could hold, I let go of that good energy to all those who had hurt me. I put out the good energy from within me as a form of emotional release, so that as a soul, I could now live in forgiveness mode without the obstruction, anger, and frustration caused by painful memories. Most of the people who came to that campfire, I forgave at the time. My mother and some of my relatives would take longer to forgive for everything. I knew there was some more healing I had to do first, in the privacy of my own space, away from everyone.

The day I left the hypnotherapist's office building after that major session of release, I went for a walk to a nearby shopping center. There I physically encountered my first soul from a past life. He was walking toward me on the footpath. Our eyes connected, and it was as if we immediately shot back to 2000 BC. I looked straight into his eyes. I knew. He knew. As he got closer and closer, a gentle smile came across his face. His eyes sparkled like a huge star, and then he passed me. I didn't look back. His energy and mine were blended. It was the most beautiful karma and soul contact I've ever had, other than with God himself, which would occur a short time later. But even though the encounter with my soul mate felt great, I didn't consciously understand what was happening. It's a bit like not knowing the 'context' of an experience. How was it connected? Why did it mean so much? Why did I feel that? Why did I know him?

After the second and third hypnosis sessions, I really felt like a new person—refreshed, light, and happy about the future and what it could bring. I was still in Sydney and enjoying the serenity of what was taking place.

One night I rang the friend, the one I'd slept with on the work trip, on his mobile phone; he'd asked me to stay in contact while I was away and had made clear that he wanted a future with me. But instead of hearing a normal hello on the end of the line, it was clear that he was in the middle of something with someone. I had interrupted something. His conversation was awkward, he was panting, and for a long time afterward I wondered if he was in the middle of being given oral sex while he was talking to me on the phone. *Betrayed again* I thought. I got off that call, sat down with pen and paper and wrote a long letter explaining that I didn't think he was the right person for me. I sent the letter; then regretted sending it—had I been too impulsive? Had I actually heard them having sex? I rang him again to ask him to destroy the letter and not read it. He sounded very unconvincing on the phone, and of course he read it, eventually. After I spoke to him the second time, I kept thinking to myself *How could anyone do that? Have sex with someone while talking on the phone to someone else? What a sleazebag, what a creep.* It was more than I could fathom.

Chapter 21

The next short period back at work and doing normal everyday living things was immensely challenging for me. I was suddenly surrounded by immoral people and hearing so much—too much dialogue, much of it useless human babble about nothing. I would listen to only classical instrumental music and not radio stations whose songs had too many words. I chose to leave the TV turned off—too much negativity, not enough good news. It was all I could do to cope with the influx of people's dialogue in the workplace. By the time the workday had finished, I needed time completely away from humanity. On the good side, that time enabled me to start living in a more meaningful way than how I had previously chosen to live. I did not speak as much, observed more, and watched diligently; I really listened to what was in people's hearts when they spoke rather than simply listening to the words. I'd always done this to an extent, but my own sense of lightness and joy allowed me to open up to people more than I'd ever done before.

When I returned to Sydney after that short break in sessions, I agreed to allow a different and longer session. I would focus on my soul, rather than focusing on memories and healing my heart. I was open to that. I knew how to get into a deep trance; I knew how the sensations in my body would go. I was comfortable and confident that I could handle that deeper spiritual work.

The session started with me sitting face up, reclined in a black leather-type chair with my feet slightly raised. In what seemed like only a short time, I could feel my heart beating strong and regularly, and yet I was outside my body surrounded by the brightest light I'd ever seen. I was encapsulated in that light and felt completely weightless. There was no sound where I was. The light created cloudiness around my whole body, but it was neither cold nor damp. It was warm, still, and soft. I felt like a peacefulness was all around me, moving inside and outside of my soul. I wasn't there as the physical person, as Nola Hennessy; it was more that my soul was there, with its form becoming part of the whole—the light, the softness, and the peacefulness. I couldn't see my physical body. I wasn't looking back to it or hovering over it. My body was somewhere else far, far away, and I couldn't connect with it.

At a soul level, I was home. That was where I belonged, and it felt right. My soul was being where it was supposed to be. It was there in Heaven where it felt at home and peaceful. In Heaven, I was powerful in a way that I can't explain; my energy was powerful, my purpose was powerful. I was not among others like me, not life forms anyway, but I did sense other spirits in that light—good spirits. It was like we were altogether as one yet still individual. There was absolutely no fear, negativity, judgment, punishment, anger, or any of the other negative traits of humanity. Heaven is all about compassion, unconditional love, forgiveness, peace, honesty, a feeling of being blessed, and deep fulfillment. I knew at that soul level that what I'd left behind on the physical Earth—the world in which I'd lived—was a mixture of goodness and the hell as it is described in religious texts and many literary works. I didn't want to go back to Earth; I wanted to stay right where I was in Heaven. That felt right. It felt safe.

The more easily my soul released to Heaven, the weaker I could sense my physical body getting. I could actually feel the heartbeat from my physical body lying in that chair, but as my soul deepened into Heaven where I really wanted to stay, the weaker and more faint my heartbeat became. The more I stepped forward into the depth of the light, the more my body weakened. It seemed like an eternity with my soul disconnected from my body. This seemed to go on for ages from my soul's perspective until finally I could hear the hypnotherapist yelling at the top of her voice, "Come back, Nola. Come back, Nola."

I could hear her yelling, and yet I couldn't comprehend why she was yelling or who "Nola" was. I was between Heaven and Earth, and it felt like I was going to be trapped in an abyss of nothingness. My soul was not empowered to choose, and it was at that exact point of realization that my soul was being directed by God that I let go to God's will. I didn't know at the time it was God making the choice, but I knew it was a higher power than me and I had no control, absolutely none. As much as I wanted to determine my outcomes at that point, it wasn't up to me. Within the blink of an eye, my soul was ripped out of Heaven and put back into my body. I lay heavy and flat in that chair, unable to move for several minutes. My heart pounded in my chest. My mind was empty and my body was numb. Each time I attempted to move part of my body or lift my head, I couldn't. I was held in the chair by a huge force all around me. It was disconcerting, but I had no fear. I didn't understand what was happening. I just had to go with the flow.

The hypnotherapist's voice was there in the distance, "Coming into the now, Nola … bringing awareness to the now." All these words and more she was using to help bring me out of the deep spiritual space. I could feel pins and needles in my feet and fingertips, then heaviness moving about my body like something surging inside, blood flowing, and energy pulsing through every part of me. My stomach was growling from a lack of food, my mouth was the driest it had ever been, and when I opened my eyes, I felt the greatest sense of disappointment and unhappiness. I wasn't in Heaven anymore. I was back on Earth. I kept thinking to myself, *I don't want to be here anymore; I don't want to be here. I want to go back.* But I couldn't get back there—not at this time.

The hypnotherapist had absolutely no idea what had happened and that my soul had travelled out of my body. She was struggling to make sense of how far away I had gone spiritually, and how she couldn't bring me out of the trance she thought she'd put me in. But that was no trance. She was thinking in the logical human-experience, scientific-evidence space, what she had been taught about the mind and memories and how that all works. But I'd been somewhere way beyond and outside that context. I didn't utter a word to her other than to say that what I felt was very different than what I'd felt before. I had to leave it at that. How on Earth would anyone ever understand what I'd just experienced or what my soul had gone through?

As I left her office, I remember getting in my car and deciding to go back to my relative's place. He was away again, and I had a key to let myself in. I thought a long time. At a deep soul level, I felt very calm, very knowing, very relaxed, and I had a sense of finality and comfort. I now knew what would happen to me after death. I finally knew for sure that Heaven existed and that Heaven is where I had gone. If I had not been good in my life to that point, I would never have seen Heaven as I did. I also knew that, for whatever reason, I was now back on Earth and had to learn to accept that. I was not fully aware of God and his part in all that had occurred.

For decades, I had seriously doubted there was a God. I'd never been religious even though I'd gone to the occasional Sunday school class. My mother had insisted I be exempt from Scripture classes at school, and I was always noted on paperwork as being nondenominational. I'd always struggled to understand how God could allow innocent young girls like Toni to suffer and die such horrible deaths or allow pedophiles to exist to hurt children. If God was what most people believed in and what religions preach about so vehemently, then God would never have allowed those things to happen. He would have been more merciful. The religious teachings, therefore, were contradictory in terms and in total conflict with the reality I knew. A priest might say, "God wanted him," to justify when a young man dies in an awful accident. In truth, that religious notion of God and what he wants is just a crock.

Most importantly, and what I didn't know then, was that I would come to learn the trueness and power of God directly through his speaking to me just a short time later. I would come to learn that God allows and encourages people to make choices, and it is with those choices that a person's destiny is largely determined. While there is always the chance that God will intervene if he chooses or allow his chosen angels to do his work under his guidance, delivering the miracles we can't explain as humans, the choices available to people exist as a result of God allowing them to exist. People will exhibit strength and tenacity, go after what they want, work hard to achieve outcomes, and be rewarded one way or another—or they will be the exact opposite. At times, they may flow between these patterns—either energetic or lazy about life. Ultimately God watches, listens, and feels what every human is about, understands what their souls need to learn in their lifetimes, and brings them to points in their lives where choices must be made. This is the one true constant in life.

Each day we make choices and manage everyday risks by making decisions. The more we learn our lessons along the journey of life, apply the learning, forgive, remain selfless, kind, compassionate, honest, and full of integrity, the less we will need to learn the next time around. It is through all those soul journeys that our soul comes to the point of clarity and perfection where there is nothing more for the soul to learn. When the soul is perfected, it finds its home in Heaven. When I finally went to bed that evening, I laid there going over the events that had occurred that day, doing my best to work out how to navigate life from that point on. I felt alone, so very alone.

As I lay there, I did everything in my power and mind to get myself back into a deep hypnotic and free state where I could journey to Heaven again. Being truly honest with myself, I knew I didn't want to be on Earth. I didn't want to be back in the hell created by other people's badness. I felt like I had no power to make things in the world right or help people be better, kinder, and happier. I wanted to be back where everything was good, sweet, and kind.

What I've come to understand is that human nature is ultimately God's greatest challenge. Human beings, through their choices, will make mistakes. Humans either learn from them or not. No human being is perfect even though some, like me, apparently, have come pretty close. God has to allow us to make mistakes so that we mature at a soul level. The longer we ignore the spiritual aspect, the longer our journey of "soul perfecting" will be. Some people may live a million lives before their soul is perfected in order to reside in God's Heaven for eternity. Some souls, like mine, are sent back to Earth either to their old physical body or to a new one to do God's work after being in Heaven for a time. This is the angel aspect that so many people misunderstand, and at times, think negatively about.

There are no bad angels despite what some literature says. Angels are pure, wholesome, and good. They can be given to humanity as a whole and also to individuals in their own right—to help them, guide them, heal them, and nurture them. Angels may not stay around forever; they are there while they're needed. An angel's job may be to help many, not just a few, and it is always God who decides an angel's obligation to him and his or her destiny on Earth. He will decide when their job is done and if they've earned the right to reside in Heaven with him rather than do his work on Earth. Angels never come back to punish. They do teach lessons, but if a person has done wrong, the angel will simply guide their learnings.

At the time of my hypnosis sessions, I didn't understand all that I do now. After I'd been in Heaven, all I wanted was to be back there. But the more I pushed to be back there, the more I felt God pushing against me. That night, to ease my intense feeling of frustration, I let go enough to get myself into a state of deep relaxation. After an hour or so in that place, I realized that going to Heaven was not my choice to make, and I let go again. In letting go that evening alone in my bed, I managed to get myself to a place of total calm and tranquility of spirit. I was starting to take more control of my own soul and its journey, and as a result of achieving that powerful sense of self-control, the memories of my soul's past lives were brought to my conscious mind that night.

Up until the time in Heaven, I felt that nothing could top that experience, but the past-life memory recall was spiritually so powerful, it brought instant answers to some long-held questions such as the déjà vu moments we have that most of us can't explain. It was a wake-up call—merely existing on Earth and being satisfied with earthly pleasures was humanity's excuse for being spiritually lazy. I had all this past information to enrich my soul and life in the now. What was I going to do with the positive power that stems from having the right information at hand?

Prior to my current physical life that began midmorning of June 17, 1957, my soul had already grown and developed in the physical bodies of three other women during their three lives.

In 2000 BC, I was a dark-haired Egyptian princess, olive-skinned, and in her twenties. I lived an easy, calm, and noble life. I lived in a large, whitish building on the banks of the Nile with three full-time attendants. My father and mother were both alive but much older than me, and I had many sisters and brothers of varying ages, all of them noble and with attendants to care for their every need. My father was very important and dressed as royalty would, the pharaoh Mentuhotep III, perhaps. My memory of that time is that he was tall, always beautifully dressed, and no one went against his word. Our lives as a family and in society were all about harmony, balance, peace, and order. I did not marry at that time and have no memory of my life later than in my twenties.

Through my life, I'd always wondered why the Egyptian robes, sandals, bosom-hugging dresses, high collar trims, elaborate headwear, necklaces, braids, jewels, gold, and the colors yellow and neutral white were always favorites. I have always chosen the finer and higher-quality things in life as I could afford them, rather than settle for something cheap and of lesser quality. And I love grapes and red wine. I have yearned to visit Africa and the Nile for as long as I have been alive. My goal is to travel to the Nile and find where I lived as a princess. I feel sure that since the connection is so strong that when I reach the physical spot on the Nile, I will instantly know that to be my soul's birthplace.

In the early 1300s, I was a long, blonde-haired, single young woman around nineteen years old who was very poor and homeless. I lived in England on the streets and do not recall having a mother, father, or any family around me at that time. I may have been an orphan. My fingernails were always dirty, long, and chipped from contact with rough things. My hair was dirty, full of debris, and matted together like dreadlocks. My body had open sores and bleeding cuts were common. The dress I wore seemed to have been on me a long time. My skin was crusty like I'd swum in muddy water and not bathed. The dress was mid-length with a very uneven hemline, had holes in it, and barely covered my breasts. It was so dirty and smelled really bad. I had a shawl made of the same woolen-type of material, but it was shredded and didn't offer much protection or warmth.

I could speak quite well, so I must have gone to some kind of school or been tutored by someone at some stage. My teeth were surprisingly in very good condition and only a little stained. My days were filled with finding food scraps to eat. Nights were very cold and wet most of the time, and I know

I rarely slept. My eyes were blue, but I had very dark circles under them that could have been from lack of sleep or a bad diet. Daytimes were not much better than the nights. I rarely felt the warmth of the sun. It must have been wintertime.

Late one afternoon, as I was finding somewhere in the street to bed down for the night, two men grabbed me by the arms and dragged me off to a dark, dirty, cold, and damp cell that had dung-mixed straw on the floor and walls made of crumbling, sandstone bricks intermixed with grey stone blocks. There was a tiny barred square hole high up in one of the walls to let some light in. The cell smelt of vomit, urine, and feces. Food was always a rank-smelling meat stew with mushy vegetable-looking pieces and usually some little stones that would have come from utensils or even off of the floor. Sometimes I would be given stale bread. I was given dirty water in a metal-like cup without a handle, but the stew was always the thing I would dry retch about whenever I could smell it coming. It was bad tasting like someone had boiled a rotten cow in it, innards and all.

For what seemed like weeks, I was kept there in the cell in shackles and with a neck collar that could be linked to the feet when necessary, until a man came to me to tell me I was going to be hanged for stealing. Apparently I was accused of stealing some bread, which I hadn't, and they had tried me and found me guilty without giving me a chance to speak up in my defense. I remember protesting passionately when they said I was to be hanged. I pleaded with them not to kill me. I kept saying, "I didn't do it. I didn't—you have to believe me!"

They didn't seem to care. I was kept in the cell for another week or so, and I remember being taken outside into a dark and misty courtyard early one morning before being led up some wooden stairs to gallows. There was a table on the upper level near the rope, and a man waiting for me. I do not remember anything past that point, but I do remember feeling sick in my stomach that no one would listen.

All of my adult life, I have enjoyed cleanliness, fresh-smelling and clean hair, sunshine, long showers, warm baths, well-cared for clothes, and well-groomed nails. Plus, I have always cleaned myself thoroughly after working in the garden. When building the mud-brick house back in the '80s and with every other home I've owned or lived in, I've always kept things neat, tidy, and clean. I was repulsed by the canned Irish stew my mother would force me to eat as a child. It tasted exactly like what I had eaten in that past life. I've always been repulsed by the smell and look of offal and vomit-smelling foods.

The lesson from that life that God asked me to address is the "speaking-up" aspect. Prior to 2002, I've always stuck up for other people who've been wronged. I was always known as an executive in business, as a mover and a shaker. Now, more so than ever, I work to right injustices and have learned to speak up when I know a serious wrong is done. I've found my voice, and people have remarked how what I say has such great impact, how influential my words are, and how I am a wave maker. I consciously use that power for only good, and I am mindful that when I'm upset about something or deeply passionate, I can send major energy waves out into the universe. I know my words are listened to, and I do my best to be careful of what I say, particularly under difficult, hurtful, or challenging circumstances.

In the late 1700s, I was the wife of a patriot officer who fought the British during the American Revolution. We lived on a country property in the north, surrounded by manicured lawns and beautiful gardens that I designed. I remember being in my mid-thirties to forties. I was tall, blonde, slim, gentle, and happy. When my husband was away fighting, I would do needlepoint, have tea parties with my female friends, and spend time enjoying the gardens and my home. Our home was two stories, with dormer windows upstairs and very tall window-filled wooden doors that opened out to a long pond that ran through the rose garden at the back of the home. There was a small but elegant winding staircase that went to the upper level and beautiful chandeliers throughout the house. Every room had fine linen and embroidered work on every table or ledge. My favorite wall ornament was a very large, gold-framed mirror that hung over the large, central sitting-room fireplace.

It was a peaceful life where my husband's word was law, and I followed his lead. I filled our home with fresh flowers, and we ate well. We were upper middle class. When I was on my own, I'd enjoy sipping tea from fine china while sitting on the veranda that was at the front of the home overlooking the entry road. I loved the gardens—an English-style setting with many deciduous trees. The home was rectangular and very regal. Horse-drawn carriages would always be going by and coming to visit. We had staff, not slaves, who were mostly older men and women. My husband's uniform was an all-dark blue-black. His overcoat was to his knees, and his breeches and waistcoat all matched. He had long black boots and a large hat. I do not recall seeing him without his uniform on.

There are so many similarities to my current life—love of chandeliers, gardens, tea, fine china, tablecloths, paintings, large mirrors, entertaining, large deciduous trees, fresh flowers in vases, and large acreages. Living back in the USA in the early 1980s was the beginning of my soul reconnection. In October 2012, I was traveling around with my friend Katie in her home state of Connecticut, and I asked her to stop as we were driving down one of the country roads. There was a home, as I remembered from the 1700s, sitting graciously behind a stone wall at the end of a long, straight driveway. I truly believe that that was close to or the actual site where I lived in the 1700s. My soul told me so, and it was like I was being pushed to get out of the car and look closer. Katie was the right person for me to be with that day during that discovery. I truly believe God allowed Katie's and my reconnection to happen in early 2012. Katie connected with me earlier in 2012 after nearly four decades of separation.

Chapter 22

With all memories erased from my conscious mind and the memory linkages to my subconscious mind severed during hypnosis, I began to re-establish the linkages starting in March 2002. As each second, minute, hour, day, week, month, and year went by more and more memories came back. The intensity of the memories seemed to grow as I grew in coping strength. When my mind was like a blank tape earlier on, God knew that I needed to have old memories resurface when I was able to cope with the knowledge each would bring. I felt like God pushed my limits so many times—sometimes too many memories would come rushing back. It was like speed-reading twenty books in one sitting and getting information overload. My brain was working overtime to filter out what could be archived for now, what could eventually be reforgotten, and what I needed to have at hand in the conscious mind to enable me to live with care and strength each day.

At other times, only one or two really big memories would come into my conscious mind from the depths of my subconscious. The memories were overwhelming at times, terrifying in their clarity, and bringing me to a new reality. Other times, the memories were so beautiful, happy, and blissful that I would just sit and cry. I had so many memories to sort back through, and many times I wished I could stop the memory recall. I know many memories have never come back. People have told me things from the past that are completely new to me. They remember where I was and what we did together, and I still to this day have no conscious or subconscious memory of the event. Even my son is shocked that I don't remember certain people, places, or events.

Most importantly, some memories came back that I just don't want to remember. I didn't realize at the time that they were coming back to help guide me in the future away from harm and toward a better life. Some were really hurtful and difficult memories; some were lovely and nurturing. That was on top of all of the brand-new experiences I was undergoing in the present, adding to my filing cabinets of memories, some archived, some forgotten.

After the Heaven experience and past-life memory recall, I returned to my home near Canberra and my workplace. Nick and I began having more contact, but my responses to him were sometimes hard to manage. He knew something was different. He was one of the countless people I had to relearn about, readjusting my thinking and actions over the coming months. It was such a difficult time for me because memories came back on a need-to-know basis. I had swift memory recall of some of the positive things but as some negative things happened, and I had no memory of coping skills, the returned memories set up real barriers in me.

Initially I feared no one, but as I experienced new things like the negativity and cruelty of others, I had to quickly work on developing new coping skills. I had to relearn essential body and soul defense mechanisms. In the early months, my autonomic nervous system wasn't functioning properly to warn me of imminent danger. My karmic intuition was redeveloping and the personal energies of some people were more than I could cope with at times. Initially I thought I was OK; I felt nothing could hurt me. I thought that the world is love, and that everyone loves everyone. It didn't take long for the reality of humanity to stare me square in the face, once again.

One perfect example of this was a work colleague who had been diagnosed with a severe and rapidly growing cancer. He knew that I had been attuned as a Reiki practitioner. He approached me to deliver Reiki to him at his home. I travelled there many times, at no cost to him or his wife. All was fine until a couple of months later when he asked me to give him Reiki at work one day. He was a senior manager, and, while I felt it inappropriate to do a private and personal therapy in the workplace, he assured me it was fine. He arranged for one of the medical/first aid rooms to be available. Based on the feedback he said his doctor was giving, the Reiki was shrinking the tumor. I was motivated to continue to help him not realizing his ulterior motives.

I delivered one hour of good solid energy to him that day in the first aid room, my hands hovering over his abdomen as

I sat by him while he lay on the single trolley bed. As we exited from the room, everyone turned to look, and at that point, I turned my head back just in time to see him smirking. Did he want people to believe something wrong had occurred? What was he setting me up for?

At that point, I started to see him in a different light. I deliberately set up another session, my last I said, in his home for that weekend. I made sure his wife was there to chat with me about his condition. We had time to have a coffee together before he got home, and I asked about his prognosis. She was delighted with what the doctors had been saying and felt sure that the Reiki had helped heal him and prolong his life. For that she was grateful. But the second he walked in his home, I could sense something was wrong at a karmic level. He had gone from being weak and insipid looking months earlier to being very healthy and strong now, and he was starting to drain me of my energy every time he came close by. It didn't feel healthy for me to support him any longer. I felt as if he were sucking the goodness right out of me at every opportunity—and he actually was.

What I hadn't remembered to do, which I'd learned when first being attuned as a Reiki practitioner many years earlier, was how to channel the good energy while still protecting myself from any bad energy coming from the patient. My soul defenses were not redeveloped enough, and I didn't fully realize what was happening until that very moment.

During that last session, which I deliberately made a short one, his wife watched for part of the session at my request. I encouraged her to do the same for him, ongoing, even though I knew she was not attuned to deliver a high level of Reiki herself.

About two years later, I was at a city park concert one Sunday and saw that man and his wife at a fairly close distance. He turned to me, and then I saw what can be described only as evil features—his eyes thin and lifeless, his ears pointy and yellowed and much smaller than before, his mouth thin and sharp, his cheeks sunken, and his face pale. He was healthy but in an evil way. I knew in an instant that the goodness he had managed to suck out of me was due to his being a dark soul in the first place—a selfish, cruel, and destructive man, insecure and incapable of real compassion.

To me, he was everything I'd ever read about bad spirits. I already knew that hell exists on Earth as a result of people's badness and negativity, rather than being somewhere you go for being bad. The vision of him that day was enough to make me realize how foolish I'd been and how much I needed to protect myself from the good energy suckers like him—the people who take and never give; the ones who arrogantly believe they have a right to things rather than proving their worth and being thankful for what comes their way. He lived for many years beyond the initial life expectancy. He had originally been given two years at best.

Due to the power of the healing that had occurred, I was keen to understand and learn the science of the subconscious mind. I enrolled in graduate studies to learn the theory behind hypnosis. I was also relearning about humanity and the severe deficiencies that so many human souls display.

If there is one analogy to how I felt it is the John Coffey character in the movie *The Green Mile*. That was how I felt about people's badness and cruelty. Every time I worked to heal people I would, inadvertently for a time, actually hurt myself by taking on some of their issues. I know how John Coffey felt, how frustrated he was that he couldn't make things right and fix what other people had done wrong—the really bad, cruel things.

The impact of negative-energy people—their inner conflicts, mixed messages, manipulative mind games, greed, and power trips—became harder and harder for me to navigate and heal from. By the time I'd achieved all the written units for my qualifications in clinical hypnotherapy, I was ready to go to Sydney for the practical and final units. Before I did that, I needed to heal again emotionally and spiritually. A couple of days before my practicums were to start, I went back to the hypnosis practitioner I'd seen before.

She was nervous for some reason; I couldn't work out why. Did she know how to take the last session when she struggled to get me back in the now? She was struggling with some inner stuff herself, and for most of that session, I felt like I was the one helping her. She was offloading all her issues on me.

What I did that day in late 2002, under hypnosis and in deep trance, was repeat a lot of the healing techniques I had used before back in March. I also did memory-regression work back to my conception and birth. Despite the lies I'd been told all my life by my mother, I was thankful that following the first rebirthing experience, I was able to relive many of the happy times of my early childhood with Dad when it was just him and me.

During that memory-regression work, I did relive many wonderful times together on the beach. My mother had told me that he was incapable of being a good father, yet I relived something completely different. I have a couple of beautiful memories of the two of us that I will undoubtedly hold for the rest of my life. In one memory, we walked down the beach in Sydney together, hand in hand, laughing, and skipping along. He also helped me get over a jellyfish sting; he was so caring and gentle with me. For years after 2002, I cried for my Dad. I wanted him back so we could do all those things over again. I missed him so much. But he had long been dead, and that would never happen. I had to grieve for him all over again to get closure on all the lies I had been told and to help ease the pain his absence had brought to my life. Many nights I cried myself to sleep saying, "I miss you Daddy. I miss you so much."

The initial impact of the first rebirthing experience was so profoundly cleansing that I felt like a new person free of limitations and baggage. I was re-energized and reborn in the most spiritually connecting way. Because hypnotherapy provides vastly accelerated healing, the latent negative impact of the session was twofold—a reduced level of defense and an increased level of susceptibility to subliminal messaging. I was in a highly dangerous mental, emotional, physical, and spiritual space, and I didn't realize it until I walked out of her office and into a shopping mall down the road.

I was going to have a cup of coffee, get something to eat, and be on my way. The negative energies I could feel coming out of total strangers all around me in the coffee shop and mall were so strong I had no idea how to protect myself. I had no idea how to fix it. What was I going to do now?

Within a couple of days, I was attending the practical and exam part of my studies in North Sydney at the Academy of Applied Hypnosis. Within a couple of hours of the practicum lessons starting at the Academy, I pulled the chief instructor aside and explained the past six months and what subconscious work I had done already over the period. I told him I was hugely susceptible to suggestion, and I pleaded with him to reverse that susceptibility under hypnosis. I felt like he was the only one who was spiritually powerful enough to facilitate that.

I agreed to have him put me into trance in full view of the class so they could learn from my situation. It didn't take long. After maybe twenty-five to thirty minutes, I felt much stronger and more able to navigate the verbal, visual, and spiritual imagery I was receiving. He simply gave me words to empower and strengthen me. I did the rest in my mind.

I have to say that he well and truly saved me. I felt like I was on a clifftop where I was either going to fall forward to an awful fate or fall back, pick myself up, and start over. I did the latter with his help. During the break time of that day in class, after my hypnosis session in full view of my fellow students, one woman spoke up amongst the crowd. She said, "You have enormous capacity to heal others. You just need to heal yourself first." I sat there looking at her and huge tears welled up in my eyes. Here she was, a total stranger who didn't know anything about me and was speaking words only those in my closest inner sanctum had ever spoken to me. I knew I had a powerful gift, and it was learning how to make that gift work for others and myself that was going to be one of my greatest challenges from that point on. While I had helped the man with his tumor, another friend with her painful gall bladder, and had healed my ex-husband of terrible tissue trauma and a badly swollen arm after his heart attack, using massage and Reiki, I needed to understand my gift in much more depth in order for me to know how to continue to help others without putting myself at further risk of harm.

Chapter 23

The few months to Christmas 2002 following the Academy graduation were challenging beyond belief. I had to rebuild the emotional, mental, physical, and spiritual defenses I had acquired and honed over the first forty-five years of my life. It was exhausting and accelerated, at times way too much for me to safely cope with. I was pushing myself in all four dimensions way beyond the norm for any human being. When I look back now to that time, I've often wondered if it was because I'd been to Heaven and had God-given, divine strength that enabled me to get through all that. There could be no other reason. From a human's perspective, I was running the gauntlet, managing life without many of the normal self-protection means at my disposal. From a spiritual perspective, I kept telling myself, "You will get through this. Be careful. Hang in there."

After returning to work, I shared a lot of what I'd experienced with a few friends and family. I later came to regret sharing this information, as some of the people used that information to work against me and bring me harm. I managed to still give up to fourteen hours a day on the job, go to the gym, play squash, and do an occasional social thing. It was at the point when I was asked, "What do you want to do with your life now?" The first thing that came into my head and out of my mouth was, "I want to take Nick, go back to Texas, find Jesse, and make a life together." I instantly remembered what Jesse's stepmom had told me—he'd married in 1989–90 and was planning on having a family.

Around September 2002, there was a turning point in my career also. While I loved my safety work in government, I felt like there had to be more I could do. Together with my staff, we had brought the government agency to a point of "best practice" in its health and safety practices and had won the accolades of other government agencies. I'd won a government award for what I'd achieved and my dedication to their outcomes. As the shift in priority within the agency began, so too did my agreement to let go. The work demand on my staff over the years had gradually been getting less and less. I was picking up some of the slack, but I could see that we were doing so well one day our jobs would no longer be required.

As a consultant, that is what one does—gets the client to a place of self-sufficiency. But as an employee earning a solid salary with great superannuation and being divorced and on my own with no second income to help fill any gaps, I was feeling reluctant to step away at that point. I did agree to a voluntary redundancy, which enabled the agency to hire a part-time practitioner to focus purely on what was left to do.

I helped find and recruit that person, a colleague in government. It worked out well at the time for the agency concerned, and I was free to move on.

The way some of the personnel in that agency handled my leaving, however, was beyond disgusting. Despite winning an award, having the ear of the CEO all the time, being highly respected by colleagues inside and outside the agency, there were a few who took my choosing to leave as an opportunity to bully and harass me, unashamedly, on a daily basis. There were even lurid and sickening phone messages left on my internal phone at work. When I'd finally had enough and after several weird and wacky phone calls that I'd answered, I reported the calls and messages to the Australian Federal Police. They were onto it immediately, listening to the voice messages left on my phone and tracing calls made to the agency. They finally pinned down three sources for the calls. I knew there were men in the agency who were interested in me, so I gave their names to the AFP. Then, suddenly and without warning, the evidentiary phone messages disappeared from my government phone. Who had deleted them?

The AFP, with no tangible evidence, was compelled to drop the investigation. Little did that agency's personnel know where I was in my spiritual journey and just how vulnerable I was to being hurt by such a negative situation. It took me months to trust anyone from that organization. I went silent when I left, and it was months before I was prepared to speak to anyone there. The impact on me was profoundly negative.

From April 2001 to 2003, I'd been renting a nice three-bedroom townhouse in NSW, just outside of Canberra. With property settlement in hand of only about $90,000, I was keen to buy a home and settle somewhere nice. All that time, I'd been happily creating a new life, having Nick over for celebrations, dinner, and breakfast. We were building a life together again as mother and son. We even went to look at a new home together, but the friend I'd had the one night stand with in January 2001 was still negatively impacting my life as was the man with the tumor.

I decided to leave the place I was living and move far away. I wasn't sure where, but the first step was to relocate myself, but keep the lease on the apartment in the meantime. Enlisting the help of my ex-husband whom I'd become friends with at the time for Nick's sake, he kept an eye on my rented townhouse. I left the region and went to Sydney for some respite with a cousin, one of the nasty family members I had forgiven under hypnosis.

Being at her home was good. It was far away, no one really knew where I was, and I felt safe. Although Nick knew where I'd gone, he later explained in tears that when I left, he had no idea if he'd ever see me again. I sent messages that I was going away for respite to other family members, and I didn't want to be disturbed. I know I was in a very upset place with all the stalking and immorality I'd encountered. I was feeling very vulnerable and unsure of everything other than the need to heal myself fully from what had happened over the last six months.

While my cousin thought I'd be boarding with her for at least six months, I only needed three weeks. She, like so many others, didn't know how quickly I could heal myself. With the knowledge of self-hypnosis now at my disposal, I used the three weeks to hone my self-hypnosis and self-healing skills, reprogram my mind to only accept and retain positive thoughts, and to discard negative thoughts and messages from my brain. I taught myself how to protect myself with universal energy, applying layer after layer of white light over myself.

At one point, in the first few days of being at her place, I was only just beginning to fully realize what work I needed to do at a deep soul level to heal myself again. One afternoon I was sitting in the living room, and my cousin's daughter came in right at the time when I burst into tears and cried out, "I don't want to be here anymore!" Unfortunately, the young lady thought I meant not wanting to be in their house. I was really saying out loud to God that I didn't want to be on Earth anymore. Humanity and life on Earth was just too awful, with too many horrible people determined to hurt and abuse others. I couldn't possibly help everyone to change. It seemed like such a heavy load for me to contemplate taking on.

Although I had easily stopped smoking after I'd let go of my emotional pain, by the time March 2003 had come, I was under enormous pressure. I'd started having a few cigarettes thinking they'd help ease the pain, but instead they brought back really negative memories. Smoking switched me back to the past. The chemicals were causing a regressive effect in my subconscious mind. All the years of not letting go of the past pain had been caused by my on-and-off-again smoking. I set my first task to stop smoking, cold turkey. I'd worked out that smoking, as temporarily good as it had felt at times during my life, was about me staying in the past and punishing myself. By that point in time, I could see no valid reason to punish myself anymore. I quit and have never looked back or had a desire to smoke since. In fact, the whole concept of being a smoker is so foreign to me that I find it hard to believe I ever did smoke.

I felt like a whole new person after I quit. I felt like I had new skin, better breath, a renewed sense of smell and taste, healthier lungs and blood vessels, increased brainpower, and mental clarity. I've never felt better. Achieving that was something my ex-husband couldn't believe I'd done. He saw I was under intense pressure from "suffering the effects of the worst case of bullying [he'd] ever seen."

The second step was to get rid of the pain I was carrying again. I rang the hypnotherapist. She was reluctant to take me through another session, but I explained to her it would be the last. I was now doing self-hypnosis every night at my cousin's place. I just needed a little external help to let go of the pain quickly. She agreed, and I went for one last time.

I explained to her that my last step after the release of pain was to find my true path for the rest of my life. I needed to help myself at a subconscious level and see inside my soul to the core of what I was meant to be doing. I knew my time in Heaven had been for a reason, and yet I still had unanswered questions. She wasn't going to influence me; she simply facilitated me getting to that deep inner place where I could find the answers for myself. I had to trust her, and I told her that her helping me this one last time would bring a great outcome.

The visit changed my life forever and helped me to see things so clearly that it was like going to Heaven again. I went into a deep trance and was presented with my spiritual guides, the three most powerful sources to guide me—God, myself, and the soul of my past life in the USA in the 1700s. The powerful messages during that soul-awakening session were different:

From God: I was to learn the greatest level of patience I had ever known. I was to remain patient no matter what, beyond when everyone else gives up.

From within me: I was to remain calm. Calm was my best place, my preferred state of being. Calmness of spirit is my strongest ally.

From the past soul mate: I needed to respect time. I was to allow myself time to heal and grow immensely strong and allow time for things to come to be as they are meant to be.

Seeing God during that session, being face-to-face with him and hearing him speak to me, was spiritually cleansing and profound beyond belief. The old doubts I'd had about God's existence and power were now all gone. He had touched me directly for a divine purpose, and that event in time changed my life forever.

Of the many scriptures I read as a child, I knew that God comes to those who are pure in their hearts—people who do not innately do or think wrong thoughts. For all of the previous decades when friends would call me a good Christian, I could only ever see that in a religious context. I wasn't religious, so how could I be a good Christian?

I have always believed that Jesus Christ was a man who existed once and was a great healer of others. I had no doubt about that. I had seen many healers myself in my own lifetime. I knew I had the capacity to be a great healer. Fundamentally, what many people had always seen in me and called a good Christian trait was my giving nature, my enthusiasm to help others without asking or wanting anything in return, my joy at the smallest of things, my gentleness, and my kindness. What the churches and religions call good Christian traits are what I just knew all along to be right, just, and unselfish.

I left the hypnotherapist's office that day without telling her what had happened then or previously. I kept it all to myself and never saw her again. We parted company under positive and enhanced circumstances. I learned much from her during the year I knew her—about the effects of hypnosis and the frailty of physical life. Big mistakes were made on her part, and she did not appreciate the strength of my mind and soul. Hypnosis paved the way for great positive change for me.

The three weeks in Sydney was a time of huge healing and strengthening for me. I even looked into becoming a nun. The only thing that stopped me was I'd have to sever ties with my son and some family members with whom I felt close. I couldn't do that. I knew that my son needed me, and I needed him. My soul told me I was right.

I hadn't gotten a full handle on the angel aspects by that stage. Being there for Nick was one of the things God wanted of me, and it took another year or so before God gave me those direct instructions. I bravely returned to my townhouse in late March 2003, packed up my home, arranged the removalist, and I was gone by the time the lease expired in April.

Chapter 24

Leaving the city in 2003 to go to the coast was exciting. The household things were put into storage, I secured a new senior management and business development role in the private sector, and I found a home to buy that wasn't far from some relatives. It was just at the point I was about to sign contracts to buy the new house that I realized something was missing. If I bought that home, I may well get stuck in that community and feel compelled to remain for the rest of my life. I was approached over the phone by an old work colleague, a very senior government official, to come back to Canberra to help her organization determine a new leadership charter and recruiting policy. I was the only one, in her mind, who could achieve that refresh of thinking that was needed. I had my removalist come, yet again, to collect my things from storage and take them back into storage into Canberra. I found a new townhouse to rent and settled into some fabulous consulting work with the government.

Unfortunately Nick was having a really hard time with life at that time, and when he visited me at my rented townhouse with his girlfriend, he let out all the pain of the couple years of me not being around all the time—not staying with his Dad, his having lost his home in the country because of the divorce, and not knowing how to deal with it. Worst of all was his intense fear of me being so different. He cried in pain that night, "You're not my mum. I want my old mum back." I couldn't explain to him all that had happened to me. He was not ready. All I could do was hold him, let him cry, let him yell, be angry, and tell him not to run in fear of the changes that he saw. It was a hugely difficult time, but I managed to get through to him that his mom was still there, that she loved him very much, and that she would never abandon him.

Shortly after that visit by him, I was the victim of a break-and-enter robbery. Nick was furious that someone had done that. The police and I knew, but without solid proof, that the perpetrators were living in the surrounding properties. Without hesitation, I paid the balance of the lease and got myself out of that place and into a rental home. I signed another six-month lease, but the next-door neighbors were the sons of the rental homeowners and had a key to the property.

As part of the lease, the sons were responsible for mowing the lawn and doing the gardening, but they had a key to the actual house. For weeks when I got home from work, there would be cushions moved to different places on the couch. My clothes and underwear were disturbed in the dresser drawers and in my closet. On top of that, they would stand on the shared driveway in front of my car as I attempted to drive in and out. They would say odd things to Nick and me on weekends—how one of their wives had divorced them because of violence. It was terrifying. I spoke to the police, and they insisted I take out an Apprehended Violence Order against the older brother. I did straight away, but that wasn't the end of the ordeal.

I'd been headhunted by Australia's Defense organization to help bring a change in health, safety, and culture to the organization. The nonsense that these guys were going on with at my home was having an adverse impact on my work, and I was very busy. I worked sometimes sixteen hours a day for Defense six days a week. I had no time for other rubbish. I took a few days off and went to court. I got the AVO upheld by the judge, and felt safe to return to the home and pack up my things. In less than twenty-four hours, I had a four-bedroom home fully packed, and the removalists collecting my possessions. I was out of the lease, and Nick and I were away from harm.

One of the key things the police told me at the time was, "It's important that you leave without fear, that you leave without running from those guys. You are taking control of your life from now on—you're not a victim anymore. Make sure once you're away that you let go of what happened there." The advice helped me to face and manage the swift and powerful change in a much better frame of mind—simple words, but powerful in their message and encouragement.

For a short few weeks through March 2004, I stayed with a young relative while I found a new home to buy. It was in a lovely country-style and gated community over the border from Canberra. I finally had a home I could decorate and landscape just the way I wanted. The house was a modern three-bedroom, two-bathroom home in a nice Colonial style.

It was also in early 2004 that I met a military officer through work and, over a few months of talking over coffee, I learned to trust him. He'd say things like "you have such an innocence about you, so pure." He liked my gentle manner, and I was likewise very supportive of him. He gave me the impression he was a likeable kind of guy and sincere. I was a totally different woman to any he had ever met before. The damage that he did over time, however, was truly unfortunate for my son and me. His deceitfulness, lies, manipulation of a situation, confusion, and ego left me with no choice than to get him out of my life. Nick watched the turmoil the "Hurricane," as he referred to himself, put me through. It took years for me to finally eliminate his negativity from my life and Nick's, and until 2009, I felt like I was in a real battle of wills with him. I had developed feelings for him at the time but as a consequence of the lies he told me, promising things he could never deliver, I found it immensely difficult to understand how someone could be such a chameleon. I learned many lessons as a result of allowing him in my life for a while and am grateful that I recognized his complete lack of integrity and realized how different our values were before it was too late.

For nearly three years, I lived in that cute little house. Nick lived back at home with me for part of that time from mid-2004 through early 2006. My mother used to visit, but the visits were getting pretty strained and uncomfortable for me and for

Nick. Because I was so calm and gentle in my approach, and she so domineering, she saw that as her opportunity for taking control of my life. When we had words about things from time to time, she would describe her style of love as tough love. No tough love is ever real love in my book or in God's.

In early December 2005, the world dropped from beneath my son's feet. Derek was killed in a light plane crash—a crash that was then the worst tragedy of its kind in the country's history. Derek was on the plane by default, flying as the co-pilot to a friend in the same flight company.

Derek's plane came down in a flaming inferno over the country outback NSW, and it was only through the friends I had made in SAR that I was able to get first-hand information very quickly, passing that onto my ex-husband and Nick. The period was deeply traumatic for everyone concerned. Nick went quiet. His father, once again, refused to allow me to say good-bye at the funeral.

Once again, I was denied by others' negative controlling nature, the right to say good-bye at the funeral of my former stepchild. He was a young man I loved like my own, had been a confidante, and I saw him through some tough and emotionally draining times in his life. I was mortified, but I stayed controlled, quiet, and positive for my sake, as well as Nick's. Nick was in a dangerous place emotionally having lost other siblings. Derek was his only surviving sibling until that time, and this loss was too great a tragedy for us to comprehend.

In staying strong for Nick, I was sometimes feeling overloaded myself. In January of 2006, I sought out a clinical psychologist to help me get through the balance of healing. I was shocked by Derek's death and very sad. After an hour and a half with her, going over old stuff from my childhood, so she had some context to my life, she reassured me I was handling things just fine. Self-hypnosis was really working well to help me heal and develop new survival skills. It was she who helped me understand the deficiencies of my mother and how having to be the parent to my own parent had made me into the person I was today—strong and capable of great compassion.

As a result of our time living together after Derek had died, Nick and I became quite close again. There were some intense misunderstandings, but his health greatly improved. I helped him to start sorting out some life hassles and find a good direction for himself not only in life but also in his career. I was starting to miss being in the country, but I hadn't decided fully whether to head toward the coast again or deeper inland.

Chapter 25

Eventually the country-style home in the surrounds of Canberra sold in the latter part of 2006, after nine months of open-home exhibitions. Nick had already moved to live with a friend, and I moved to a tiny town near the ten acres that I'd found in a beautiful part of NSW. The acreage was close enough for me to commute to Defense each day. Life was looking much better despite some negative memory recall and times of heartache. I focused on the future. I could landscape in a big way and create an oasis like I had in the Snowy Mountains region. I thought one day I might get a horse or two and use that home as the base for my future consulting company.

I knew that it was only a matter of time before I would leave working for the government as an employee. I found the public service in Australia to be way too controlling and suffocating an environment to ever make anything of my career. They wanted to dictate someone's future and not allow the person to take control. I had only a few years to go before I would qualify for long service leave. I'd made some fabulous contacts right across government, and with my CV fully revealed, there was little chance of me ever gaining enough promotions. Everyone I worked for was already way junior to the roles I'd previously had, and they found it difficult to have someone so senior working for them. My time in the Australian public sector was starting to come to a logical end.

While in the rental home at Bowning, I penned my first book, *No Boxing Allowed*. On the eve of my 50th birthday in June of 2007, I e-mailed the transcript to my old work colleague and friend, Major General Ian Gordon, who was heading up peacekeeping forces in Jerusalem for the United Nations at the time. I asked him to write a foreword if and only if he liked the work and supported what I was saying. On the morning of my fiftieth birthday, I received back from him the foreword that he penned. I was flabbergasted, dumbstruck, and overwhelmed. I never thought someone would value what I'd written so much. It had seemed to me that all I had learned, the hard lessons in life, and the patterns that I'd found in myself and others wasn't going to be of interest to anyone but me. Ian Gordon's words changed all that.

I'd sent the early manuscript off to a major international publisher. They asked me to increase the content, and they were very keen to promote it and have me do book signings internationally. It was after Ian's foreword that I felt ready to resend it to them. Unfortunately, while the initial editor was delighted to walk forward with me in publishing and promoting the book on a global scale, by the time the second version was ready, he'd left or moved elsewhere in the company.

I had to liaise with another editor, and he mishandled the manuscript so badly. I was stunned—he'd given it to a senior "spiritual leader" in Sydney to read and learn from. How dare they—that was my work, my story, my spiritual guidance, and my philosophy they were plagiarizing. I had no trust for the big players in the industry for a long time after that. Ian then offered to publish *No Boxing Allowed* through his own small publishing company, but I felt like I needed to take control of where my books were headed. I knew the books would, when the time was right, become the foundation for the consulting work of my future company. I had to be deliberate and careful with my choices.

My fiftieth birthday celebration was a mixture of elation and disappointment. Some of the people I wanted there couldn't come. Others whom I felt obliged to invite were there doing their best to take over that special event for me. I was feeling very empowered in my decision to minimize contact with my mother after the hypnosis sessions in Sydney and the adverse experiences I'd had with her coming to my home near Canberra in recent years. My son needed me more, and he was my priority. Our relationship had come under enormous pressure due to my leaving his father, and I needed to fix things between us.

On and off for the first fifty years of my life, I'd wondered why my mother constantly pushed me away, yet when it suited her, she controlled my every movement and appeared to want to have me around. She would be critical of me in private yet glowing of me to others. She was an extraordinarily dominant disciplinarian, always telling me I had to work harder and harder. She said that my efforts weren't really good enough, then she would say I deserved the best—completely mixed messages. She used me as child-slave labor, robbed me of my childhood, and was rarely genuinely satisfied with my performance in life. She fed me mixed messages all the time and was downright cruel when it suited her.

In October 2007, I was sitting relaxing in the quiet, rural rental home in Bowning. My new home on ten acres above Yass, NSW, was still under construction. I visited the building site at least every day, and I had begun to landscape with Lambertiana Pines from North America. I had many daily challenges but was feeling strong and hopeful about the future. I was just five years into what I called my new life, but I was still having old memories surface in my conscious mind at regular and sometimes rapid intervals. I was sitting relaxing on the sofa in my rental home when I had a memory recall that put me in high spiritual self-defense mode for months. The memory instantly brought answers to many long-held questions from my life.

Even though I'd been through the rebirthing experience, I had more memories surface about my birth that day like a second rebirthing. I remembered hospital noises in detail; the clanging of wheels; the feeling of being rolled forward; a dark, tight passage; and the flickering of lights intermittently. I remembered hearing the words, "Get this baby out of me. I don't want it," coming loudly out of my mother's mouth with such force and venom. Everything went still for me as a baby.

I was stunned, even as a child unborn, hearing those words spoken by my biological mother in the middle of giving birth to me. I remember the brightest light right in my face and a hard pressure all around me. It was over, and I was born. There was no one to hold me and kiss me; no one was close by. I have no memory of being held and cherished for being born. When I had that memory recall of what my mother said while she was giving birth, I was stunned. I thought to myself, *There you go, Nola. That's your karma right back at you. You were the one not wanted.*

I know for a fact that in this life or in a next, what you do or say wrong in one life, if left unfixed or without attempt to repair, will come back as a lesson to teach you later in that life or in the next one. The worse the error is that you make, whether deliberate or not, the worse the lesson later. I must admit that I'm glad my karmic lesson about being her unwanted daughter came back at a time when I was strong enough and emotionally resilient enough to handle that truth. Any earlier could have been the wrong time, and I may not have handled things quite the same to protect myself so vehemently from my mother's negative impact.

Chapter 26

Life on the ranch was physically exhausting at times, yet so fulfilling in many ways. From early 2007, I started to project-manage the building of a large, four-bedroom home with magical 360-degree views. I landscaped the three-acre area directly around the home with a significant border of beautiful pine trees and developed some gardens. I built retaining walls, had fencing put in to divide the paddocks from the residential area, and really cleaned up the property so that it was a pleasure for people to come and visit.

The builder went bankrupt the day the keys were to be handed over in May 2008. It took three days for me to get the keys from them. I'd paid all the money, and yet the building supervisor wouldn't hand over the keys. The build costs had blown out 40 percent on top of my original budget, the time to build had blown out six months, and without a promotion in sight, I was living life very close to the line. For three months before moving into the home in May 2008, I lived in a local motel at a huge financial cost.

By the time I'd moved into my new ranch home, I was doing everything in my power to get out of the public service for good. I had really cemented in my mind, through all that I'd had going on in the last decade or so, the view that only a few possessions are needed in order to survive in life and create happiness. That enduring sense of happiness comes from simplicity, acceptance, and remaining forever hopeful.

At many times over the period from 2006 to 2008, I'd felt things at a universal energy level speed up and then significantly slow down. I sensed a stalling happening on many fronts. God seemed to be holding things back, and I didn't know why. During a portion of 2008, I felt God nudging me forward. Jesse's name would appear everywhere. I would see men in the street, and they would be the spitting image of Jesse. I was not sure why these things were happening, but I noted the signs. I knew time would reveal what else was coming.

I'd begun to pen my second book, *From Pre-Menstrual Syndrome to Positive Mental Attitude*, which was ultimately published in late 2009, shortly after *No Boxing Allowed*. I was happy being an author and enjoyed sharing through this medium. The second book was difficult to write at times, but it was essential that I get that stuff out of me. I wanted others to benefit from my mistakes, my experiences, the lessons I learned, and share the PMS cure I'd found.

In seeing so many men do the wrong thing by me, I often wondered if God was pushing me down a path to Jesse that may lead to heartache again. As far as I knew from Jesse's stepmom in 1989, Jesse had been married for almost twenty years.

I'd search the Internet to get a clue from time to time but then let the search go. It all seemed pointless to me. I know God, in one way, was giving me what I had been asking for over the decades, but the images and reminders of Jesse were confusing and challenging. Feelings for Jesse were stirring again, but my feelings for the Hurricane and the concerns I held were not resolved. I really was very hesitant about men in general and concluded that all men must be the same.

By the beginning of 2009, I was quietly searching the Internet again for a way to connect to Jesse. *Maybe things could be different*, I thought. Finally around April, I found Jesse's stepbrother through an e-mail address. I e-mailed a basic introduction with enough information that if he was the right person, then he'd know. The reply was almost instantaneous, very welcoming, and happy. It contained photos of Jesse with his teenage daughter. Jesse was copied on the return e-mail. For the next few hours, I wondered what the heck to do: *Should I contact Jesse? But he was married! Why had his stepbrother copied him on the e-mail?*

A bit of traffic went back and forth between the stepbrother and me until it was revealed that Jesse wasn't married and never had been. I had no idea what to do, but with all of the good memories of my time with him being so fresh in my mind and the misunderstandings and other people's lies never straightened out, I wanted to set the record straight at least from my perspective. I wrote him a fairly long e-mail explaining things and correcting any possible misunderstandings. It took a while for Jesse to reply, but he did reply explaining that his stepmom and stepdad had passed away. He seemed pleased to hear from me and was careful in how to explain those recent deaths. It created a great sadness in me that I'd never see them again.

Things were not so great in Jesse's world at that time, and with God nudging me to reconnect, I again wrote to Jesse. I explained that I'd found some joy and love after my marriage ended, and I asked if Jesse would be friends with me. I felt that he could help correct the damage created in recent years by inconsiderate and ego-driven men, and I also wanted to share with him all the plans I had and the experiences I'd had in the spiritual realm. He was an intelligent man; I believed he would understand. I trusted him to eventually tell him about Heaven, although I wasn't sure how. From his first two e-mails, I felt he was the perfect one to be a good friend when I needed one the most.

In my new life journey with all the career, family, and men-related disappointments, I sometimes doubted God's intentions and hoped to find some reprieve from what seemed like God's constant control over my destiny. I hadn't yet come fully to terms with the Heaven and angel aspects as much as I knew I had to, and I couldn't speak to anyone about it. My first thought always was, *Who would understand?* Even though I wanted to, I couldn't bring myself to share that with Jesse, not yet.

In the meantime, I was getting ready for a big career change. In early 2009, I took a long break on holiday and some much-needed sick leave from the public service. I'd decided to sell the ranch and move to the coast. Earlier in the year,

I'd commenced discussions with Lockheed Martin's CEO in Australia. There was every likelihood that I would join them mid-year, and I did in the August of 2009. I was making my planned exit from the public sector very public knowledge. I established a five-year plan for myself at Lockheed after which I planned to establish a consulting company again in Australia.

However, the struggle with God to get out of the public sector was a battle of divine wills. By my birthday in June 2009, I was intensely frustrated by the constant delay. I felt like I would get stuck in the government. The morning I received official word of Lockheed and my escape from the public sector, I felt a strong pressure like movement over my heart. It was like God had run a firm hand from top to bottom of my heart in a wavelike motion. The wave on my heart came a nanosecond before the phone call. In my heart, I knew God was giving me what I really wanted and had worked hard for. He was stroking my heart. I've never felt anything like that wave before in my life. I can't fully explain how great it felt other than it was profound. God had made me work so hard, and I was being rewarded. I must be doing things right despite all my doubts, frustrations, and heartache in recent years.

Once I'd left the government and was on my first trip to Melbourne as an international consultant to Lockheed Global, I was thinking about how Jesse's life deserved to be better than he had experienced. I knew deep down he had a good heart and was a good man in so many respects. He was loyal to many people when he could have easily turned his back; he'd been loyal to me in many ways.

He'd obviously suffered greatly in his life, but enough was enough. I believed he deserved a break. I also knew that I had the right temperament to handle him now. I had changed so much as a result of the healing journey. Later that year, I e-mailed Jesse offering him another chance to get to know each other again. If it didn't work out, then we could just part ways and leave it at that. What I was offering seemed pretty straightforward, and God also nudged me to hang in with it. It didn't take long for me to realize that Jesse was not interested in talking directly with me—not even by e-mail. I wasn't told why; the e-mail replies just stopped or were non-existent for months.

For almost eighteen months, I had quite a bit of contact with Jesse's stepbrother. His wife and I swapped letters, she sent me pictures, and I sent pictures to them. I had a real connection with her at that time. I heard all the news of the family and was genuinely interested in being a support to Jesse. I wanted to be his friend, and if something came of that later, then great. However, Jesse wasn't communicating with me.

Around 2010, my first boyfriend made contact with me and told me he'd gone to where I lived in Sydney in 1981. He missed me by a couple of weeks—I'd moved to the USA. All these decades later, he found me. His long marriage was under pressure, he obviously wasn't happy, and he was reaching out to the woman he claims to have always loved. I thought it might be nice to reconnect and be friends; however, I sensed he was wanting more in the long run. I was in love with Jesse again, and that love for Jesse was a genuine barrier. I told him

I was "In love with another man and always would be." I let him know that there was no "us."

I learned from that subsequent contact from him that the first love you have can really set the tone for the rest of your life. However, the love at that time may not be one that should be repeated later. People grow and change, and it is the sum total of their life experiences that brings them to a point in time. The most important thing I didn't have a chance to communicate to him when he reconnected with me was that if a marriage or relationship isn't working, then a decision has to be made to end it, uninfluenced by other people or other things. After a relationship has ended, it is important to rediscover yourself as an individual, to heal from past wounds, and to determine what you really want before committing to a new life with or without a new partner. Leaving one partner for another without time in between is, with few exceptions, a very risky place to put your heart and soul. I did it once rebounding from Jesse to Bill and nothing good came of it other than my son being born.

Chapter 27

By the end of 2009, it was clear God had other plans for me, and the five-year plan I'd documented involving Lockheed was accelerated forward. I was not in control; he was. God was creating opportunities and choices for me, pushing me hard to establish my corporate structure, and go back to consulting in my own right full-time. By November of 2009, I was back in Defense consulting in quality and governance. I was having a great time. My books were published, and I was beginning the long journey of marketing involved in that.

For the next two years, I consulted to the government. At the same time, I had the ranch up for sale and was doing exhibitions, listing the property with agent after agent. I had three full property sales fall through over an eighteen-month period. It was devastating and financially draining. There was no money around, and we were amidst the global financial crisis.

In early and mid-2011, my company secured a place as a preferred supplier on two government panels. We were well and truly on our way. I bit the bullet and decided to drop the price of the ranch. I wanted to get out of there for good and be on the track to company growth in a more ideal and travel-conducive location—on the East coast a couple of hours south of Sydney. My books had already begun winning awards in 2011, and in March, I was honored with unexpected recognition from Rotary International as one of their "Inspirational Women."

Between late 2009 and November 2011, what transpired between Australia and Texas was a whole bunch of communication and miscommunication and adverse influence by people with selfish agendas. I did not keep secrets, but I didn't really reveal the Heaven and angel aspects fully to Jesse at the time either. I believe now that that was a mistake.

Despite attempting to sever ties with Jesse's family in mid-2011, in November 2011, I was compelled through circumstances related to my book marketing and business development to detour through Texas on my way to Miami. One of Jesse's friends used that time to discredit Jesse in every way possible, telling me his truth about things because he said, "It is for your own good."

The so-called friend of Jesse's not only violated my trust by making passes at me on several occasions, he pushed for photos with me, pushed for me to listen to his music and to his stories, and pushed for me to go to his residence, which I calmly refused to do. I knew the instant I laid eyes on him that his energy was evil, perverted, and destructive. His motives in wanting me to see Jesse in a different light were so clear I was not only upset, I became strongly defensive of Jesse.

However, as a result of me choosing to share with Jesse the horrible things I'd been told about him, Jesse chose to get angry with me. Once again, I felt Jesse believed another's lies before the truth. Since then, I've held the view that Jesse has to start seeing things for what they really are. I kept telling God to let me let go of the love I had for Jesse; I wanted out. It was a dysfunctional situation, and I couldn't see a positive end. The extent of people's lies and deceit would come out; people can't be that immoral without someone finding out what they're really like and what they've said at some point in the future. I didn't need to be around or say anything. They would dig their own graves, in time.

In December 2011, I started to really let go. I wanted no more of God's divine plan with regard to Jesse. There were too many people wanting to control the outcomes to suit their own agendas. I wanted no part of that kind of life. I'd left that life behind years and decades earlier.

By early 2012, I had a solid buyer for my ranch. I'd taken it off the last agent. They were all useless in getting a sale, and I had strong interest in selling the house through doing exhibitions each weekend myself. By the time the sale came through, I'd dropped the price by $120,000—none of which I could afford to lose but necessary. I had to be on my way. For eighteen months, over 80 percent of the house had been packed and stored in a storage container at the coast. Prior to each unsuccessful sale, I'd taken more and more things to the storage unit. I was done living out of boxes with the barest of furniture in a hollow-sounding house, and I had started to forget all the lovely things I owned and hadn't seen for nearly two years. The ranch was no longer home. There was zero emotional attachment, and I'd found a new home. I'd been patient long enough and had endured enough; I wanted to be gone to the coast.

By that stage in life, my view of men and my future had really started to cement. I've never counted how many or few men had been in my life; that's quite irrelevant and really doesn't matter in the bigger picture anyway. I now value the fact that I'm healthy, disease-free, knowledgeable about love and of sufficient skill level in the sexual sense that life is satisfying for me. I've learned more about what I like and don't like, and what gives me pleasure and what doesn't in every context in the last thirteen years living alone without a partner in my life than I ever learned in the forty-five years before that. I have nothing to prove to myself, let alone anyone else. My few but genuine male friends treat me well, and I still receive wolf whistles from strangers much to my surprise. I enjoy the company of many interesting and different men and women, and I have a positive view of life as the foundation for all that I do. While many men think that going years without intimacy with the opposite sex means something is wrong, celibacy has been a virtue and not a deficiency. I am stronger emotionally and more comfortable with who I am. I never was and never will be a sex-for-sex's sake woman.

Chapter 28

In late March 2012, the ranch sale was finalized, and I'd moved. By April 20, I'd settled in at the coast and had the keys to my new home. The job of settling in to the new home, keeping the company operations working, and my own consulting work going forward was a huge load, but I was motivated to keep on going. I could see good things in sight. I'd signed with a new publisher in January 2012, and they guaranteed things would be different than the first time. My books were being republished that year—relaunched in every respect.

With the new publishing contracts in place, winning many awards, and global marketing underway, I was ready to travel to the USA in June 2012—the start of my book tour and many promotional events that year. I saw one old girlfriend again that trip and during that visit with her for the first time since 1989, we laughed about many things. It was a special reunion, and even though we have not remained in contact since, we did talk about Jesse and those times back in the 1980s. When I told her what I had been told during 2011, she enlightened me to some other truths about the so-called friend of Jesse's. She then turned to me and said, "I've got a surprise; he's on his way here."

I blushed, my heart started to race, and I felt very uncertain. She took back what she said as a joke, laughed, and to this day I don't know why she played that trick on me. She knew full well that I had fallen back in love with Jesse over recent years. I met her daughter that day and during an earlier conversation with her, I summarized my life and my feelings on men and love. What I said then still holds true today: "The last time I made love was in Texas with Jesse in August 1982. The last time I had sex was about a decade ago. There's a big difference between making love and having sex. He's the only man I ever truly loved."

While Nick and I were busy building the company's strength in Australia during the June through December period of 2012, I had a successful first leg of my book tour in August through September accompanied by Nick for three weeks. It was his first time out of the country. I took a week out to show him Texas, and I introduced him to my old friends there. However, by October 2012, when I was due to return to the USA, in the face of all my normal work and home life activities, God started putting me under enormous emotional pressure again regarding Jesse. I attended a major media event in New York in mid-October, and every day I was in the presence of another attendee who was identical to Jesse—same look, same height, same everything. It was like Jesse was there with me the whole time.

In the middle of a book-signing event in Pasadena, California, I had a few minutes to browse the shelves of books near where I was sitting. I took one pretty book from the shelf, *Weddings on Any Budget,* and I thought to myself, *This will be good for when Nick gets married one day; there are lots of good ideas.* I looked up, and there was Jesse's name in my face on the spine of a wedding book. At various airports, I would see Jesse everywhere—his face, his body form, his name. I was really feeling overwhelmed and due to go to Jesse's hometown in just a few short weeks. What was I going to do if I saw Jesse? Was God preparing me for some divine intervention? Once again, I felt out of control of my fate, and it was more than I could deal with. At that point, I wished I'd never gone to Heaven.

My emergency trip to a hospital in Austin, with what I believe was just a bad case of food poisoning, was the beginning of the end of my trip in the USA in November 2012. My closest girlfriend was my helper again at that time, so loving and caring. I was grateful for the care I received by paramedics and hospital staff, but the drugs they gave me were excessive and more than my drug-free body could cope with. I had wanted to spend more time in Austin with her and her family, but my visit was cut short. I felt really unwell with odd palpitations and dizziness.

After my return to Australia in November 2012 and after fully recuperating, I repositioned my company to publish my first two books and let go of the other publishing house—a positive move for the future. With a significant amount of media attention, professional interest, many awards, and glowing testimonials, I am now totally focused on developing strong educational material from the books so that I and others I train can teach these principles to teenagers and adults for generations to come. What I've written in my books is the truth, and I know it's through truth that we gain the right to stand in the light.

For these last few years particularly, I've felt a bit like a pawn in God's game. It is hard to describe the universal energy struggle God and I have sometimes. I literally feel his energy push me in a direction, and if I don't want to go there yet, it's like a wind roaring at my back to push me forward. He can hold me back relentlessly until he's ready, or he can push me hard forward when it's his time. It's just awful. The energetic forces and telepathic-style communication we have between us are beyond this Earth—it's like a giant magnetic force that I have to push to get through just to get him to agree sometimes. As I've often said, I feel like I mainline to God every time I open my mouth.

The hardest part for me is when I get to the height of my frustrations and exasperations with him. I think to myself, *I'm just an angel back in my old human body. Knowing that is hard enough to deal with. Leave me be! Please!* I really feel like even though I'm an angel here living as a human, God has stripped away my rights as a human. It's like I have no place, in his eyes, to be less than perfect. I have no right to err as a human. I'm expected to deliver so much more than humanity. It's an enormous pressure, and I keep telling myself, *God is only giving you what you are strong enough to cope with.* I wish I could get just a little slack. Believe me, I've asked God for that bit of slack quite often.

It's been unfortunate that Jesse never came to know that God wanted me to be the one to help him achieve his dreams and the success he had worked so hard for. God instilled in me the importance of holistic forgiveness, and coupled with the patience that he'd given me a double dose of in my new life, he knew Jesse would thrive.

However, I never communicated the angel aspects to Jesse properly. I'd skirt around the issue; I'd sidestep what was very hard for me to fully talk about. I'd only tell Jesse in letters and e-mails what I thought I should say. I basically chickened out of explaining the full extent of Heaven with Jesse until it was way too late.

Everyone else's meddling, influence, and agendas had pretty well stuffed up what would have been quite beautiful. If only I'd told Jesse the angel aspects in the same way I'd told my own son, Nick. Jesse and I had always deserved privacy to talk through things, and we didn't really get it. For all of God's pushing me toward Jesse, to get him to open up and communicate and see what is possible, I have only one thing to say to God. In the beautiful words of George Strait, "You can lead a heart to love, but you can't make it fall." God has his divine plan, but I believe Jesse deserves to be allowed to live his life the way he really wants with the people he chooses. His choices don't involve me. My working strongly against God's wishes to fulfill Jesse's choices may have created a spiritual conflict in me for a while, but I feel much better that what I did was right for Jesse.

In mid-February 2013, I gave Jesse, the greatest love of my life, his freedom ticket. It's been a divine battle, and my heart has been crushed, but Jesse has had his wish fulfilled. That's what is most important to me. That is what true love means—putting the other person's needs before your own. Soon after I let go of Jesse, my mother's soul connected to mine. Almost every time I opened my mouth from mid-February to February 28 when she passed away, I could hear her speaking. She must have been wanting to reconnect with me. The news of her death was something I knew, at a spiritual level, was coming. It's funny how the more she pushed, the more I backed away from her soul's connection.

On April 26, 2013, I was given visibility of my mother's will, drawn up at a time when she was in the poorest physical and mental condition. It was as clear as the full moon that day how little she valued me as a human being or as her only daughter who had loved her unconditionally for more than fifty years. With her now gone and her soul no longer channeling to me, I feel totally free. I am free of her pushing from her deathbed, free of the possibility that she will again work to destroy what I have, free of the concern I always held that she would repeat her antics as the mother/monster-in-law nightmare, and free of tough love and the heartbreak that brings.

Epilogue

My relationship with God is an interesting one that I've described before as mainlining. I take that phrase from the heroin-addict boyfriend I knew once. Heroin addicts mainline to get a quick fix. The analogy to God is not so much about the quick hit. It's that when I speak to him or write down what is important to me at any given point in time, I know that he's listening. He'll give me signs—tangible, unmistakable signs such as physical sensations in my body that show me he's present, helping when he chooses, and pushing me to be discerning and careful in my choices. My wisdom has come directly from the effort I've made to understand his power and the experiences he has made me endure.

I believe it's essential that humans learn to release a desire to control others, and also learn that relinquishing control of a situation doesn't mean that a person loses their power. A soul's journey to perfection involves learning and requires constant change. When a person lives their life without really changing all that much or changes for the worse, their soul's path to get back on track, erase the deficiencies, and begin the journey to purity and perfection will be all that much harder to travel. A soul's journey is as unique as the physical body through which it lives. Nurturing and improving your soul at all times and under all conditions achieves a level of peace that is palpable to every human being. Our soul mates exist throughout humanity, on every continent, and in every color. Discovering them is a good thing for your soul, and can bring a huge sense of closure to those déjà vu moments experienced in life.

We have the power to correct our soul deficiencies at any time during our physical life, and in order for us to complete our journey to perfection, it's critical that we understand the opposite, nonperfect state. Our souls all start imperfect, and it is through mistakes, lessons learned and applied, and more lives that we can remove and temper the imperfections and change at a spiritual level to become perfect and earn the right to be in Heaven.

The deficiencies of competitiveness and egotism can be replaced with acceptance and letting go of your ego. Selfishness can be replaced with generosity, sharing, and selflessness. Compassion, caring, kindness, and gentle love must replace cruelty and harshness. Loudness must be tempered into quiet self-control where an ego is no longer required. Exaggeration can easily be replaced by balanced thinking and tempering self-talk. Intolerances and prejudices have no place in life and should be removed to allow for acceptance, tolerance, and understanding. Fear can be replaced by acceptance, contentment, and calmness. Jealousy, as useless as it is, must be replaced by acceptance, that what exists for us is OK, that equality is a better frame of mind, and that the removal of fear can be achieved through gaining self-intelligence.

Likewise impatience needs to be replaced by patience and calmness. Addictions will destroy your soul if you let them; therefore, strong self-control, acceptance, self-love, and giving to others will help you overcome those tendencies. Dishonesty must be replaced by honesty and integrity. Avoidance, while easy at the time, must be replaced by ownership, accountability, and strong self-control. Greed, humanity's greatest flaw of choice, must be eliminated through selflessness, giving to others, and always sharing. Finally, the need for control over others or everything must be replaced with acceptance, strong self-control, living without an ego, and without fear.

At a spiritual level, I've learned a great deal over the last twelve years. When we have purity of heart, we can see ourselves so clearly. We look with open eyes at our own deficiencies and can more easily determine how to improve. Purity of heart is about being full of compassion—for self and for others. In 2002, I realized that in my previous life I had an ego to satisfy. In my new life, my soul has journeyed beyond needing that ego. I have, at a soul level, learned to give to myself the recognition for being a good person. Those who choose to know me as the deeply spiritual person I have evolved to be understand why my selfless acts are so important to me. They understand why I bounce back to happy despite every challenge and negative situation that comes my way. They know that if I were left alone on this Earth, I would still survive and thrive. Through my own soul's journey, I know that anyone can journey to the point of not needing an ego, and yet still function quite profoundly as a member of our greater humanity.

Success is not measured by money, status, power, or possessions. The effort you put into perfecting your soul will be, ultimately, how you are judged and the true success of your life measured. There are not always two sides to a story. When an individual wrong is done, it's done by one person through their actions and inactions, words both spoken and unspoken. The response to that wrong is owned and chosen by the other. Everyone has a choice to make when they respond. Making a wrong be owned by the recipient of the wrongdoing, as well as the perpetrator is simply humanity's excuse for nonownership of a state of being or a situation. It is exactly why there is so much injustice, unfairness, and betrayal existing in our world. We don't always get what we deserve, and we don't always receive what we expect that we should. We are sometimes made to endure far more than seems right. However, to know in your heart that you have done everything right through the whole journey of life and have acted selflessly in all your decisions, your soul will be the one at peace in the end.

I still wake up every morning, breathe in and out, give thanks for being alive and healthy, and continue to be the best I can be in everything I do and say. I make sure that my soul is nurtured, and that I can live up to God's divine standards. I engage in outdoor activities as much as possible. I bought a one-man kayak from Nick late in 2012, and the first time I did so well I was shocked. It was like I'd always kayaked. I love walks on the sand, being beside the beach, and traveling and being in the countryside.

I love what I do with my companies and the business activities, the people and engagement aspects, and achieving wins. I currently balance work with activities like photography, gardening, the orchard and vegetable garden, watching good movies, travel, writing, taking Nick's dog for a walk, and dining with Nick whenever I can.

My soul-deep love of Texas and the USA and my feeling of having "left Australia for good" back in May 1981 was the key reason for the strong connection I formed with Texas and the American people in the early 1980s. That connection with Texas—the love of the outdoors, an adventurous lifestyle, the music, the country dancing, the smells, the food, and the multidimensional way of life—draw me back time and time again. I have no doubt that I will live there again one day soon. My work with my consulting company and a desire to share that work with America is what keeps me motivated to that end.

Most importantly, I remain grateful for the lessons I've learned, as hard as they have been sometimes. I've shared my soul in this autobiography. I hope that in some small way, it illuminates lessons for you or inspires you to a better outcome. There are so many others who have lived a harsher life than mine, and they have my deepest empathy. If I can bring value or healing to your life, then my life on this Earth will have been a most worthwhile nanosecond in humanity's journey.

About the Author

Nola Hennessy rose from a childhood of severe constraints to lead her global consultancy Serenidad Consulting®. *The Peace Angel* chronicles that journey. Her international and multi-award-winning books, *No Boxing Allowed* and *From Pre-Menstrual Syndrome to Positive Mental Attitude*, are the foundation for her life's work, professionally and personally.

A Fellow of the Australian Institute of Management and a member of the UN Association of Australia, she has been involved in volunteer work since childhood, culminating in her being an award finalist and one of Rotary International's Inspirational Women for 2011 and a winner of *Focus on Women Magazine's* "Women of Impact" Awards in 2014. Her work in growing alliances around the globe continues daily as she travels anywhere she's needed, and gratefully accepts challenges and opportunities as a means to facilitating positive change.

www.ingramcontent.com/pod-product-compliance
Lightning Source LLC
Chambersburg PA
CBHW040320300426
44112CB00020B/2822